Home Sweet Jerome

Death and Rebirth of Arizona's Richest Copper Mining City

Diane Sward Rapaport

Johnson Books
BOULDER

Published by Johnson Books
a Big Earth Publishing company
3005 Center Green Drive, Suite 225
Boulder, Colorado 80301
800-256-5830
www.bigearthpublishing.com

Cover and text illustrations by Anne Bassett *(www.jeromeartistannebassett.com/)*
Cover and text design by D.K. Luraas
Author photo by ML Lincoln
Jerome sign on back cover: Bob Petley photo. Image courtesy Jerome Historical Society.

9   8   7   6   5   4   3   2   1

Library of Congress Control Number: 2014932889
ISBN: 978-1-55566-454-1

The following are excerpts from articles written by Diane Sward Rapaport about Jerome that have been published in other periodicals.

"An End and a Beginning" and "How the Jerome Historical Society was Formed," *The Jerome Chronicle*, Winter, 2012
"Rescuing Jerome from its Ghosts," *The Journal of Arizona History*, winter 2012
"The Best Little Ghost Town in Arizona," *Southwest Passages*, 1993
"Paul Nonnast: House on the Edge of Time," *ArtSpace*, 1988
"In Search of the Mother Lode," "Mining in Jerome," *Sedona Times*, 1987 and 1988
"Company with a Social Conscience," *The Sedona Times*, February 3–February 9, 1988
"The Tailings Near Tuzigoot, Fear, Fact and Fiction," "A River Worth Fighting for," and "Fire on the Mountain," *The Tab*, 1988
"A Real Cowboy Lady: Katie Lee, Authentic 'Country Western,'" *Sing Out Magazine*, 1992
"Prologue to Home Sweet Jerome" and "Ghost of the Gun," *3QR The Three Quarter Review: Poetry & Prose*, May 2012

Vignettes have appeared on Diane Sward Rapaport's blog: http://homesweetjeromedrapaport.wordpress.com/

The Home Sweet Jerome vignette, "How to Get Rid of Grasshoppers," was published as a guest blog on author Kristy Athens blogsite, http://www.getyourpitchforkon.com. Kristy's book, *Get Your Pitchfork On: The Real Dirt on Country Living*, is a great introduction for people that are thinking of moving to the country and are ill-prepared for the practical realities of doing so.

The Dutchman's Palace," by Katie Lee, *The Journal of Arizona History* (Summer 2013). Excerpt reprinted with permission of Katie Lee and the Arizona Historical Society.

Any Internet references contained in this work are current at publication time, but the publisher cannot guarantee that a specific location will continue to be maintained. Please refer to the publisher's website for links to author's website and other sources.

Printed in United States of America

Contents

Acknowledgments

This book was written with the love, encouragement, and helpful advice from a wide circle of family, friends, cowriters, editors, and publishers.

First and foremost, I want to thank Walter Rapaport, my husband, for forbearance and love throughout this project and my children Kamala Joy, Michael Sward, and Max Rapaport, grandchildren Aaron and Robin Austin, and my first cousin Denise Rapp. They were always interested and supportive. Some of the best stories were sparked by their memories.

Thank you to members and former members of the Jerome Town Council, members of the Planning and Zoning and Design Review Boards, and Jerome Volunteer Fire Department. Thank you to the old board and current board members of the Jerome Historical Society that have been helpful throughout. Particular thanks to Lew and Mimi Currier, Richard Martin, Jane Moore, Rosemary Shemaitis, Peggy Tovrea, and Doyle Vines from the town of Jerome; and Jay Kinsella, James Tomlinson, and archivist Colleen Holt at the Jerome Historical Society. They patiently answered questions and found documents in their archives and plied me with photographs and encouragement. They gave interviews and answered odd questions when I called with "Do you remember ...?"

I thank John McMillan, Margaret Mason, Mickey Peterson, Russ Wahmann, Laura Williams, and the venerable historian Herbert V. Young, with whom I worked as a board member and president of the Jerome Historical Society and have since passed away.

Countless friends in Jerome and the Verde Valley have graciously granted me formal interviews, some more than once, including Ron Ballatore, Anne Bassett, Barbara Blackburn, Hank Chaikin, Mimi and Lew Currier, Nancy Driver, Wylci Fables and Jore Park, James Faernstrom, Richard Flagg, Omar Fray, David and Susan Hall, Berta and Paul Handverger, Barbara Henley, Carmen Kotting, Katie Lee, Jo van Leeuwen, ML Lincoln, Lee and Nancy Louden and Nina Louden, Anthony Lozano, Sr., Anthony Lozano, Jr., Karen Mackenzie, Sherry McMahon, John and Iris McNerney, Richard Martin, Charles Matheus, Jane Moore, Julie Perkins, Paul Nonnast, Scott Owens, Andy Peterson, Ellen Smith, Robert Sandoval, Gary Shapiro, DeDe Shamel, Glen Stockton, Caroline Talbot, Henry Vincent, Doyle Vines, Amy Waddell, John Waddell, Billy Watt, Mike and Roberta Westcott, David White, and Kathleen Williamson.

Thank you to geologists Wayne Ranney, Paul Lindberg, and Paul Handverger, who enhanced my understanding of the geology of the Jerome area and its mines.

Thanks to my Jerome buddies that commented on my blogs and corrected them, including Diane Bell, Roger Davis, Susan Dowling, Greg Driver, Nancy Driver, Leigh Hay Martin, Richard Martin, and Jane Moore.

Special thanks to artist Anne Bassett for her magnificent cover illustration "Jerome on Acid" and for the use of her black and white illustrations. In 1982, Anne began documenting the intricacy of Jerome's visual heritage during its period of restoration and growth. Her pen and inks and watercolors have drawn a great deal of praise: *"I am enormously complimented that people from around the world have told me they came to Jerome after seeing its charm in my drawings."* Like many residents, Anne participated in town politics, first helping draft its comprehensive plan, participating in the Planning and Zoning Commission and Design Review Boards, and serving as a member of the Jerome Town Council. She helped start the Jerome Artists Cooperative Gallery. You can visit her work at: *www. jeromeartistannebassett.com/*

Another special thanks to photographer Bob Swanson of Swanson Images whose photographs appear in this book and who has helped illustrate many of the articles I had published in various magazines. He has been a wonderful friend and encourager. You can visit his work at *www. swansonimages.com*. Much appreciation goes to my long-time friend and graphic designer Julie Sullivan, who provided early layouts for this book in the late 1980s, when it was conceived primarily as a photo documentary.

Particular thanks go to my friend ML Lincoln, filmmaker (*Wrenched*) and photographer who spent a lot of time trying to get me to relax for an author photo and to her son-in-law Randall Bellows III for helping to convert them to black and white.

Special thanks to the organizations, illustrators, photographers, and friends who contributed the use of their photographs and illustrations: Jerome Historical Society, Jerome Fire Department, Ron Chilston, Pam Fullerton, Richard Kimbrough, Katie Lee, ML Lincoln, James "Q" Martin, Richard Martin, Ellen Jo Roberts, Gary Romig, and Michael Thompson.

To readers of particular chapters who provided much helpful advice and some editing: Kristy Athens, JoAnn Braheny, Lew Currier, George Glassman, Colleen Holt, Alan Kishbaugh, Claire Larsen, and Richard Martin.

To Richard Flagg and Pam Clark, who opened up their homes to Walter and I when we returned to Jerome to finish my research.

Thank you to artist Pam Fullerton, who took the trouble to go through her garage to find a poster she illustrated for Jerome Instrument Corporation and scan it for me.

When my husband and I moved to Hines, Oregon, I joined The Writers Guild of Harney County (formerly Harney Basin Writer's Group). Members listened to some of my early Jerome stories and encouraged me. I particularly thank Myrla Dean, the group's moderator, who turned to me one day very early on and asked, "Who are you writing this for?" I was stumped. "It's perfectly okay to just write for yourself," said Myrla. That broke some dam inside me and I started writing the stories that became a blog, some excerpts of which are included in this book. Another very special thanks goes to guild member and published novelist Marjorie Thelan. She showed me how to format and organize this book and encouraged me ever forward.

Thanks to WordPress for helping me find an audience for *Home Sweet Jerome*.

Gracious thanks to Richard W. Etulain, Professor Emeritus of History at the University of New Mexico and author/editor of more than forty Western history books, who gave a workshop in Burns, encouraged me, and steered me to the University of New Mexico Press, which encouraged me even more by writing one of the most gracious rejection letters I've ever seen.

A very warm thank you to George Glassman for his final edit of *Home Sweet Jerome*. He has been editing my writing for over twenty years and knows how to make it smooth and judicious.

And last, but not least, thanks to my publisher, Johnson Books, a subsidiary of Big Earth Publishing, for accepting this book, and especially to Mira Perrizo for her enthusiasm and edits.

Prologue

If you are a student of Jerome's history, as I am, you study ghosts, the people that came before you, that grew up in the house you live in, planted the crab apple and apricot trees you eat from, plundered the mountain where you now walk your dog and try to figure out what they created or destroyed has to do with the present and future.

If part of you is a romantic, you would sense the ghosts that amble about Jerome's streets, souls that did not depart for some other job, another ugly mining town, who died too early, got too old, parked their memories inside their homes so their emotions could tug them back to hard times, better times, family times. These are the ghosts that can't bury Jerome in their hearts and haunt the people that live there today.

And if you have studied Buddhism or Taoism, as I have, you understand that the spirits of animate and inanimate life are everywhere, and if you shut yourself off from them you shut down part of your humanity and separate yourself from the essential nature of the universe.

Introduction—
The Town that Refused to Die

Jerome, Arizona, is a town that died and was reborn several times in just over a century. It was Arizona's richest copper city. It became a celebrated ghost town after the mines closed in 1953. It was a hippie and artist redoubt in the 1970s, as notorious and beautiful as Taos, New Mexico, San Miguel de Allende, Mexico, and Mill Valley, California. Now, Jerome is visited by over a million people a year.

I arrived in Jerome in 1979 with my husband, Walter, and two-year old son, Max. All we could see was a beautiful view to a valley and the pastel buttes beyond as we approached from the steep winding road above. We came to a sign, "Entering Jerome." No town. No houses. My eyes panned the 180-degree panorama that was almost 80 miles wide.

Another few curves and suddenly we were in the town, with houses to the edge of the highway. Most of the town could be captured in a glance. It terraced down to the neighborhood called Deception Gulch.

Another half mile, another curve, and we were on Main Street.

There were no parked cars. No gas station. No motel. We stopped. Walked around a little. No people. No open coffee house, just a few closed curio shops and some big buildings either boarded up or without roofs. There was a lot of rubble, and a steep copper-colored mountain with no vegetation. The whole town looked like a gigantic, cockeyed marionette strung up by telephone and electric wires. It created the illusion that if the wires were removed, the whole town would topple down the hillside. The stillness was eerie.

I could scarcely imagine that 15,000 people had lived here in the early part of the twentieth century when Jerome was an industrial giant that held two of the richest and most famous copper mines in the Southwest.

It was equally difficult to imagine Jerome after large-scale mining had stopped in 1953 when this large city became a village that became celebrated as Arizona's most famous ghost town. Photographs taken in that period show a dilapidated, deserted town—a movie set waiting for a script.

We were anxious to leave the urban bedlam of the San Francisco Bay area and find a less harried way of life. Now, we found ourselves in a crumbling village of about four hundred people and a stupendous view.

1

We got back in our car and drove up and down a few steep streets. Finally, we noticed a familiar "No Turkey" sign in a window. We stopped and knocked on the door. Out stepped our friend Barbara with a big cheery welcome. This was to be our home for the next eighteen months.

Barbara was a hippie friend we knew in San Francisco. Her Jerome home was the center for big parties—movable feasts that started with joints and coffee in the morning and continued to festivities that might end up in one of the nearby canyons. She had a generous heart. Everybody was her friend. "I never met a stranger," she would say.

It did not take us long to meet the 250 or so eccentrics and artists of Jerome. Everyone seemed so exotic that I felt caught up in a carnival.

It was a poor carnival though, and many residents struggled to live. There were few resources to repair leaky water and sewer lines, collapsed retaining walls, buckled streets and sidewalks, and abandoned buildings. People struggled to make a decent living; jobs were scarce. I was lucky. Twice a week, the owner of one of the Main Street shops paid me to dress up people in antique clothes and take their photos. The pay was twenty-four dollars a day. I had not earned that little money since high school.

However, there was a strong current of idealism, resourcefulness, and euphoria that strived to rescue Jerome, and I got swept along. That current wove in and out of my life for the next thirty years.

As board member and president of the Jerome Historical Society, my job was to help maintain a historic community, and I helped to uphold the new ordinances adopted by the town in 1980 as a member of the Planning and Zoning and Design Review boards.

I wrote brochures and newsletters, operating manuals for software and scientific instrumentation, grants for various town organizations and artists, and promotional articles for my new publishing and public relations company. I was known as the town scribe.

I became privy to the ups and downs, fortunes and misfortunes, dreams and ambitions of a quirky patchwork of rebels, scoundrels, heroes, and artists. I heard stories of preposterous dimensions: the ten-dollar sale of Main Street in the 1950s; large pot gardens in the mountains around Jerome; and the theft of a large amount of money from the Catholic Church. New dramas occurred almost weekly: fights over the Company Hill houses, the discovery of azure-colored toxic water in some of the ditches, and a mayor who used her position to try to rent a prime space in the Hotel Jerome. There was a huge drug bust in October of 1985, and the town made *The New York Times* on January 21, 1986, with the headline "Ghost Town That

Was Restored To Life Is Now In Uproar Over Raid For Drugs." These stories were part of Jerome's new history after the mines closed, and I set out to chronicle them.

Home Sweet Jerome is the story of Jerome's rescue after 1953. It was a town that was too stubborn to die, despite many difficulties. Many colorful stories and interviews are woven into the historical narrative.

I am sure that my choice of people and my perspectives of the events that shaped Jerome's history will differ from others that lived here during this period. Jerome is a town of four hundred people and a thousand opinions. It's a kaleidoscope of colorful myths, tall tales, and ghost stories.

Most of us that have lived here, however, agree that we share a supernatural attachment to Jerome. It will always be home sweet Jerome for us.

Overview of Jerome

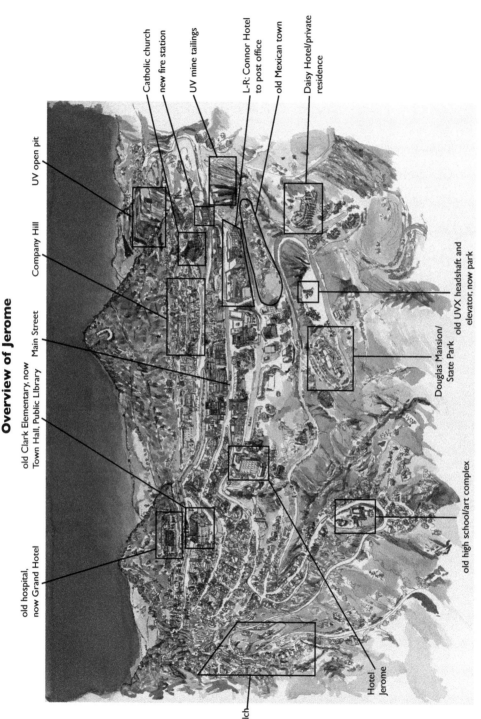

old hospital,
now Grand Hotel

old Clark Elementary, now
Town Hall, Public Library

Main Street

Company Hill

UV open pit

Catholic church

new fire station

UV mine tailings

L-R: Connor Hotel
to post office

old Mexican town

Daisy Hotel/private
residence

Hotel
Jerome

Gulch

old high school/art complex

Douglas Mansion/
State Park

old UVX headshaft and
elevator; now park

"*Jerome on Acid.*" *Drawings by Bassett, www.jeromeartistannebassett.com.*

A Tour of Jerome

Entering Main Street, Jerome. Coming up from Cottonwood and Clarkdale, you'll eventually make a left turn and come to a stop sign. The big "J" on Cleopatra Mountain will be right in front of you. Drawings by Bassett, www.jeromeartistannebassett.com.

Jerome Park

At the stop sign, you will also be facing the beautiful town park. Drawings by Bassett, www.jeromeartistannebassett.com.

Connor Hotel, Jerome, Arizona

Bassett © 96

Turn right at the stop sign and the beautifully restored Connor Hotel will be on your right. Drawings by Bassett, www. jeromeartistannebassett.com.

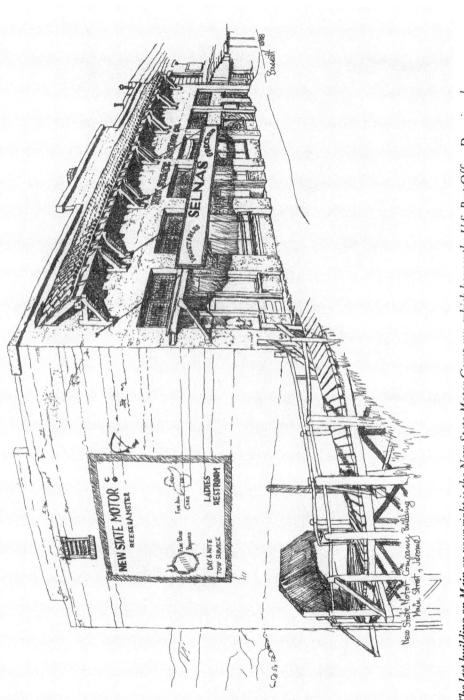

The last building on Main on your right is the New State Motor Company, which houses the U.S. Post Office. Drawings by Bassett, www.jeromeartistannebassett.com.

Turn left, and the first buildings *you come to are the Police Department, followed by the Clinkscales building and* The Turquoise Spider. *Drawings by Bassett, www.jeromeartistannebassett.com.*

Block Four, Main Street, Jerome

The next set of Main Street buildings after you pass Clinkscales and The Turquoise Spider is dominated by the Boyd Hotel, owned by the Jerome Historical Society. The upper floors are apartments, with views from the balconies that are world-class. Drawings by Bassett, www.jeromeartistannebassett.com.

The Flatiron building and, across the street from it, the Hotel Jerome that houses the Jerome Artists Cooperative Gallery. Drawings by Bassett, www.jeromeartistannebassett.com.

Central Hotel Annex, Jerome

Bassett ©'86

Directly across the street from the Hotel Jerome is the Central Hotel Annex and the Central Hotel. Drawings by Bassett, www. jeromeartistannebassett.com.

One
Jerome Collapses to a Ghost of its Former Self

"Ever seen an acre of copper?" Jerome historian Herbert V. Young once asked me. "That's what there was in the yards of the smelter in Clarkdale, Arizona, when Phelps Dodge Corporation bought the United Verde Copper Company in 1935. Ninety-million pounds of it—nine million ten-pound bars."

At the time, Young was the old and venerable archivist of the Jerome Historical Society who had worked for both mines. I was the newly elected president of the Historical Society and curious about what Jerome was like as a mining Mecca.

Jerome's two great mines, the United Verde Copper Company (UV) and the United Verde Extension Gold, Silver and Copper Mining Company (UVX), operated within a mile of each other.

The United Verde comprised the open pit and buildings just outside of town and below Sunshine Hill. William Andrews Clark, the robber baron who was reputed to be richer than Rockefeller, owned the UV.

Clark was the financial buccaneer that brought the West into the industrial age. Because of him, Jerome became one of the richest industrial mining cities of the West, the center of northern Arizona. He owned thirteen mines in Butte, Montana (but not the Anaconda, which belonged to Marcus Daly), and a large beet farm in California.

He and his banker brother Ross built the railroad that connected Los Angeles, California, and Salt Lake City, Utah, and purchased a large valley ranch that the railroad passed through. The valley eventually became the center of the great city of Las Vegas, Nevada. The county was named Clark County in their honor.

James Stuart Douglas was the owner of the UVX mine. Its shafts were located on the land below the beautiful white mansion that Douglas built for himself and his family. James Douglas, his father, became president of Phelps Dodge and Company in 1908.

Loy Smelter—the United Verde copper smelter that was built on Cleopatra Mountain to process the very rich ore underneath Jerome. The houses on the hill were torn down when the smelter was moved to Clarkdale in 1916 so that open pit mining could begin. Courtesy Jerome Historical Society (PH2.6.2).

Clark and Douglas built homes for their executives and separate smelters in Clarkdale and Clemenceau (now part of Cottonwood) in the valley below Jerome. Separate railroads carted ore from Jerome to the smelters. Douglas built a tramway to cart ore down to the valley. They competed for laborers and were respectful, but wary of each other.

Jerome was one of the nation's largest copper producers and one of Arizona's wealthiest cities. Large quantities of zinc, silver, and gold were also mined. Legend has it that the value of the gold and silver was enough to cover the expenses of mining the copper and zinc. These mines made billions of dollars in profits. United Verde Copper Company (1889–1935) and its successor, Phelps Dodge Corporation (1936–1953) mined: "2.5 billion pounds of copper [1.25 million tons], many millions of pounds of zinc, 50 million ounces of silver [1,562.5 tons], and 1 million ounces of gold [31.25 tons]."[1]

United Verde Extension (UVX), nicknamed the Little Daisy (1915–1938) mined: "3.9 million tons of copper, 221 tons of silver, and 6.25 tons of gold."[2]

The mines were fabled among geologists throughout the world because of the high concentrations of ore they contained. The UVX averaged 12 to

13 percent copper to the ton, with some concentrations as high as 45 percent, which made it one of the two highest-grade deposits found in the world. The UV averaged 5 percent copper to the ton. The majority of copper mines worldwide average less than 1 percent copper to the ton.

The city underneath Jerome led to its wealth aboveground. At the Jerome State Historic Park, a three-dimensional display shows a city larger than the one that used to be above it: eighty-eight miles of tunnels wind deep below the surface. Thousands of men worked in those tunnels. They fed the life of the city above and gave it its great wealth.

When mining stopped, Jerome's underground city became a lifeless catacomb that contained what was once the town's lifeblood. Aboveground, the once teeming city shrank to a small village.

Rawhide Jimmy: Being Wrong and Right at the Same Time

The Douglas family has an illustrious history in mining circles. James Douglas, Jr. began working for Phelps Dodge in 1880 at the age of forty-three. By 1908, he had transformed it into a Fortune 500 company and had become its first president and then CEO. He was known as the father of Arizona's copper industry and was regarded as one of the foremost metal and mining authorities in the world. [3]

His son, Jimmy Stuart Douglas, managed some of the Phelps Dodge properties in southern Arizona, where he was nicknamed "Rawhide Jimmy," because he used rawhide to protect the rollers on mining equipment, such as cable car inclines. [4]

He frequently visited Jerome. It is not difficult to imagine him staring at United Verde's old smelter and watching Clark's rail cars ship out six million pounds of copper, zinc, gold, and silver a month. The open pit did not exist. He saw the black lava formation known as the Hickey that sat adjacent to the smelter and another portion of lava hundreds of feet below, where it had down-faulted during an earthquake on the ancient Verde Fault located between the upper part of Jerome and Cleopatra Mountain. He noticed that the smelter was located on the upper side of the fault line.

He thought, what else down-faulted? The answer must have come in a flash: a large chunk of the United Verde ore body must have sheared off during the earthquake and lay buried underneath the Hickey formation.

Douglas' theory prompted him to raise $250,000 from friends and investors. He bought the wedge of property that became the United Verde Extension Mine (Little Daisy) in 1912 and started operations. William Andrews Clark, owner of the United Verde, had scorned the wedge, as did other geologists.

Douglas found no copper, gold, or silver during the first eighteen months. Still, he remained extraordinarily optimistic in a series of letters that he wrote to his father. [5]

1913: "We are about to sink the new shaft ... it is quite possible that we may find a mine there twice as big as the United Verde. [There is] justification of the expenditure of the necessary money to get down to the 1200 foot level."

January 1914: "I am as nearly positive as can be of our finding ore somewhere in the UVX ground."

As of January 1915, no ore had been struck even with shafts that extended down 1,400 feet. "Still a great deal of work to be done," wrote Douglas to his father.

By then, Douglas began to have a few doubts and started slowly cutting jobs. But once the mining bug is caught, it does not end until the money is gone. The sheer strength of his convictions and the lure of striking it rich carried him along. "You never stop a drift until you go ten feet farther" is an old miner's adage.

Miners finally struck a thick vein of copper in March 1915. It was richer than anything that had ever been seen in Arizona. "Thirty-five percent ore" wrote a jubilant Douglas to his father. Douglas had just struck it very rich. A year later, Douglas wrote to his father, "It seems almost like a fairy tale."

During its first year, the mine produced $10 million worth of copper, silver, and gold, of which $7.4 million was profit.

Geologic investigations of the Jerome area in the 1970s proved Douglas correct in his assumption that the area containing the UVX ore body had down-faulted, but they proved him wrong in his assumption that the ore body had sheared off from the United Verde ore body. Geologists found them to be two separate ore bodies that were entombed for 1.8 billion years in the ancient undersea volcano that became known as the Cleopatra formation. [6]

Douglas' discovery of his fabled ores "was a matter of serendipity and very good luck," commented Paul Lindberg, a noted geologist who has worked for several of the largest mining companies in the world and did extensive exploration work of the Jerome area in the 1970s.

James "Rawhide Jimmy'" Douglas died in 1949. He never knew that he had been simultaneously right and wrong.

The Big Landslide

Three blocks of Jerome's commercial district and the residential area below it collapsed in 1937. The ground shifted and caused a slide that began at the east side of Main Street, where the Bartlett Hotel stands, and ran down to the buildings on both sides of Hull and Rich Streets, areas that were devoted to automotive and metal trades along with thirty boarding houses and private residences.

Streets, sidewalks, and buildings sunk a few inches and buckled. They developed cracks and listed, like ships on the sea. The post office and the

The rubble left behind after the large landslide of 1937, caused by mine explosions, collapsed three blocks of Jerome. Courtesy Jerome Historical Society (J-1990-327).

Ritz Theater collapsed entirely; other buildings were condemned by the town and demolished.[7]

The concrete structure of the old jail separated from the wooden structure to which it was attached. During the next fifteen years, residents watched the jail slowly creep across the road, a hazard for cars to sneak around. It eventually came to rest 224 feet from its original location and earned the name, "Sliding Jail."[8]

The town of Jerome and the owners of the buildings blamed the slide on mine blasts and sued both mines.[9]

Jerome historian Herbert V. Young called the blasts man-made earthquakes. The blasts ranged in size from small dynamite blasts of 54,000 pounds to explosions of 260,000 pounds, "the equivalent of six standard freight car loads." Some of the blasts occurred right underneath the landslide area. The explosions caused shifts in the Verde Fault, which is just above the business district and separates the 1.8 billion-year-old Cleopatra formation from the other formations below.[10]

The mines agreed to settle and paid out a total of $53,500 to building owners and the town of Jerome, not enough for owners to recoup their investments or the town to repair damage of the water pipes, sewer lines, and fire hydrants and to clean up the rubble.

After the settlements were made, UVX bought up many commercial properties, including the property that was leveled by the landslide, the block that housed the Fashion Saloon and Bartlett Hotel, and some buildings that had suffered some cracks across the street from the slide, such as the Boyd Hotel and Sullivan Apartments. John McMillan, one of the people that lived in Jerome then, said UVX did so because they wanted to avoid any new lawsuits.[11]

Paul Lindberg, the geologist who helped conduct the new investigations, had a more acerbic explanation. "When you build a town on top of a substrate of clay, and lubricate it with rain water and leaking septic systems, even if mining had never taken place, the town would have slipped. In the big landslide, mining got blamed."[12]

Equally, a town built over an even bigger underground city both of which exist on a steeply pitched mountain in an area that is ringed with faults is not a great formula for stability.

The Closing of the United Verde Extension

Jimmy Douglas closed the United Verde Extension Gold, Silver and Copper Mining Company (UVX) in 1938, because the high-grade copper ore had played out. Afterward, many of the mine buildings were demolished. The tram and the railroad carried away the tools, the large earthmoving equipment, and ore carts to other mines. After the trains made their last trips down the hill, the tracks were taken up. The large elevator shafts below the Douglas Mansion, a few office buildings, and tailings piles remained.

The Little Daisy Hotel, a monument to the largesse of Douglas' reign, was de-roofed and gutted to its walls and arches but not before vandals had broken in and carted away furniture, bathtubs, and fixtures.

The Honeymoon Cottage, the mansion built for Lewis Douglas, Jimmy's son, and the beautiful homes that were built for the mine executives were locked and the people that lived in them moved away.

When UVX discontinued mining, Douglas transferred the assets to the Clemenceau Mining Company, a public corporation, which then issued stocks to former UVX stockholders. In 1947, the Clemenceau Mining Company transferred all remaining assets to Verde Exploration Limited (Verde Ex), a public corporation that issued its own stock certificates. It owned a great deal of property in Jerome, from the top of the Gulch to Mexican town, the land below the post office (the old Mexican barrio), the property and some homes on the east side of Highway 89A from Gulch Road up to the edge of town, and the buildings it bought on Main Street.

The Little Daisy Hotel was originally built by James Douglas to house executives and visitors to the United Verde Extension Gold, Silver and Copper Mining Company; later it became a miner's hotel. In the 1940s, the hotel was de-roofed and gutted. It was a playground for children, a great party hotel for weddings and barbecues, and a favorite place to draw, paint and photograph from. It was bought and restored as a baronial mansion in the 1990s. Courtesy Jerome Historical Society (2003-076-039).

Homes that had been built on Verde Ex property paid a small amount of "land rent."

The Douglas family retained ownership of the Douglas Mansion, the homes built for the executives, and the Little Daisy Hotel.

Mexican employees pulled down hundreds of homes in the Mexican neighborhoods between the Douglas Mansion and the old cemetery. There was little evidence after 1953 that those neighborhoods had ever existed.

Phelps Dodge Discontinues Big Mining

Employment at the Phelps Dodge Copper Company (PD) mine plummeted along with the drop in the price of copper after World War II. Miners were laid off and executives moved to other mines. Little by little, the large excavators, bulldozers, and trucks that were used at the open pit mine were loaded on railcars and taken away. Those who were still employed knew with great certainty that it was only a matter of time before the mine would shut down.

Phelps Dodge told residents to move out of the fifty-five Victorian-looking Company Hill houses above Main Street and the United Verde apartments in 1948.

The company auctioned off most of the private residences it owned with the provision that they be torn down for salvage or carted away. This included thirty-six homes that were located on Perkinsville Road next to the tennis court and a few homes on Sunshine Hill opposite the open pit. These were substantial homes with hardwood floors and stucco exteriors. The flat streets just off Perkinsville Road gave easy access to the flatbed trucks that carted the houses to Prescott, Clarkdale, Cottonwood, Williams, and Lake Mary. The charge, which included fences and corrugated sheds, to put a house on a flatbed was between $750 and $1,500.[13]

Phelps Dodge closed another thirty houses that were located about 500 feet below the tennis courts and behind Sunshine Hill (called the 500-level). They boarded up the Company Hill houses and the United Verde apartments. The hospital was closed in 1950. In late 1953, PD sold two prominent commercial buildings on the condition they be demolished: the handsome four-story T.F. Miller building, which held the commissary, and the Ewing Transfer building. Verde Ex tore down the Con O'Keefe building, which was next to the T.F. Miller building, which PD said was "pushing dangerously" against it.

The City Empties Out

Between 1937 and 1953, five thousand neighbors waved goodbye, some never to be seen again. "Everybody was always leaving," Robert Sandoval told me. He was born and grew up in Jerome. "Even before the mine closed, people were finding new jobs and moving all over the country. People would move out their furniture, pile it onto trucks with the kids on top and wave goodbye. We all tried to keep in touch. We had built special bonds in Jerome and helped each other out. We were like family with our neighbors and friends. Everyone missed Jerome terribly."

It was not just the people that disappeared. It was the mining operations and the businesses they created. Little by little grocery stores, bars, restaurants, hotels, brothels, shops, and the opera house closed and were boarded up.

As the town emptied, school budgets shrank and so did sports and arts programs, field trips, vocational education, and building maintenance. Clark Street Elementary School was closed in the fall of 1953 and the school district gave the building to the town of Jerome. Mingus Union High School was closed down.[14]

Two Methodist churches and the Episcopal Church were closed, but Father John still held Mass in the Holy Family Catholic Church.

By 1953, less than a dozen businesses were open. There were two bars, one Chinese restaurant, and two small grocery stores uptown. There was a mortuary near the elementary school, a small grocery store and gas station in the Gulch, and a pig farm out on the hogback.

Only three hundred buildings remained in Jerome at the end of 1953.[15]

Who Stayed?

Two hundred and nineteen people, 87 of them children, stayed behind, uncertain of what the future would bring.[16]

They occupied seventy homes and apartments.

There were thirty-three families with children, and six of those families had grandparents that lived with them. Seventy-six people were of Mexican origin, two were African-Americans, one was Chinese, and twenty families were mixtures of Slavs, Slovenians, and Croats. The rest were Irish, English, and various European.

Some stayed because they loved Jerome. "Heck, where else could you find a world-class view out your window," said Jimmie Thomas. "All we had to do is sit up here an' look outside to see its magnificence. Do you leave the hometown and go look for something that might not be there or do you make the best of what you have?"

Some were stuck with no place else to move: retired miners, seven widows and a widower with children, and some families that cared for elderly parents. Those that worked for the mines had meager pensions, and a few received social security checks.

Some still had jobs. Six people were employed by Phelps Dodge and United Verde Extension to manage the properties. The high school principal lived in Jerome, as did two teachers, a cafeteria worker, the school bus driver and his wife who gave private piano lessons. The town of Jerome hired two part-time night watchmen. The post office employed two people.

21

One person was volunteer mayor and another was volunteer town manager, city magistrate, city treasurer, tax collector, and town clerk.[17] Many of the able-bodied men were volunteer firemen. Jerome became what was perhaps the smallest incorporated town in America.

Burton Young, the son of mining historian Herbert V. Young, wrote me a letter about the people who stayed behind in 1953. "[They] found themselves in the middle of a rapidly decaying conglomeration of old buildings which by almost any definition would soon become a genuine 'ghost' city. The Jerome residents, plus a few former residents, my dad included, were motivated to try to salvage something from the relentless decay that was oppressing them. The few die-hards that remained did so because they considered Jerome a very desirable place to live. But to be a viable community they needed a sustaining source of income."

That income would not find its way to Jerome for another twenty-five years.

Robert Sandoval: I Didn't Have Much of a Childhood

"My father died of a heart attack the year before the mine closed. I had just turned ten. My dad's social security provided basics for my mother, Esiquia Sandoval, and my brothers and sisters: Carmen, Jesse, Josie, Beatriz, and Michael. My mother stayed a housewife.

"After my father died, I didn't have much of a childhood. My brother and I were always working. We were a big family and the social security didn't go far. Just before the mine closed and after my father died, some of us poor kids that had lost our fathers would steal coal from that little cubbyhole near where the old fire station used to be. It was a dump shoot for the coal. We would sometimes chop firewood or do yard work for some of the widows that still lived in the barrio and that gave us some spending money. We got wood from Peterson's sawmill and then we had to chop it up. We always had to have plenty of wood in the wood box or we could not go anywhere. My mother was very strict.

"We lived in the shady part of town. In the winter we would only get about three hours of sunlight. We slept downstairs and sometimes my brother Jesse and I would sleep together to stay warmer. When Jesse joined the service, I would take the mattress off of his bed and put it on top of me for more warmth. There was no heat down there and it could get really cold. We'd stuff holes in the walls with cardboard. Upstairs, we had a wood stove in the bedroom and a wood stove for cooking. Some people used oil-burning stoves, which were pretty efficient, but stinky.

"In 1953, when the Miller building was demolished, my brother and me cleaned bricks. They were stacked on pallets, 500 per pallet. We got a penny a brick. We'd

Robert Sandoval and other kids playing on the roof of Company Hill houses in the mid-1950s. Photo by Art Clark from Ballad of Laughing Mountain. *Courtesy Jerome Historical Society (2003-076-047).*

use a small hatchet to get the mortar off. We got so we could clean a pallet an hour. I remember ten to fifteen kids cleaning bricks, even some girls. Everyone had their own pallet.

"We also made money by tearing down the houses of our neighbors. That's where we got our school money. Me and my brother stripped the roof, pulled the nails, sorted and categorized the lumber, and people would take their lumber with them, and whatever they couldn't use, we used for firewood. We were paid $100 a house, maybe $150–$175 for the bigger ones. It was a lot of work for two kids. We tore down about ten to fifteen homes. We worked after school and on weekends."

Anthony Lozano and the Pig Farm

"My family tried to leave Jerome maybe in 1948, maybe 1950, before the mine closed. I was four or five years old. My father made some kind of makeshift living quarters on his flatbed truck for my mom and the family and put some kind of military type wood stove in it. He went looking for work in Nevada—in Ely, Pioche, Elko, and Tonopah—

lonesome places. Somewhere along the way he picked up a dove and put it in the cab with us and the dove stayed with us as we traveled. Somewhere near Christmas, we went to a window display in Tonopah, Nevada, and my father said, 'This will not work. I'm taking us all back to Jerome.' He took us back and left us there. 'I'll be back in a few months,' he said. Maybe about six months passed, maybe more, he was back. We were sitting on the porch eating melon from the Varella store in the Gulch. He informed my mom he'd been there for three days fixing the service station just down the road and announced he was going to open it. He lived in a little room in that gas station so he could keep it open 24 hours; he would sleep in between cars and trucks. The station had two pumps, one an old hand pump, and he made a meager income.

"In those days, just survival was difficult and we focused on making ends meet as a family. The philosophy was that no one lived better than another. The family pooled everything in one place.

"I was eight years old when I started helping my father in the station to repair tires and worked there until I was nine or ten. Interstate 17 opened in 1956 and that killed a lot of traffic in Jerome and the gas station business. To get to Prescott, Jerome, and Sedona from Phoenix, you'd have to come through Wickenburg and up to Prescott, then over to Jerome and through the valley.

"My father also believed in helping others. He provided a 'way station' for field hands that were picking crops and moving from state to state. They could stop and recover before going on. In those days, there were more Anglo field hands than Mexicans. There weren't a lot of them, but they could find shelter here in what used to be an old schoolhouse in the Gulch. My father kept rice and beans for them and some linens. It was a point of welcome for them. The only thing he asked was that they wash the linens before they left.

"I didn't learn about this until I was much older. Not many people knew. He did that until the interstate came.

"In 1956, Jimmie Cambruzzi sold me a little sow and sixteen piglets; I got in the car and went to Phoenix with fifteen piglets. Maybe I was eleven or twelve by then and I already knew how to drive. I sold all of them. A while later, I bought Jimmie's little hog farm out on the hogback and he showed me what had to be done. We shook hands on a deal. He said I could pay him $320 when I could. That was the real word—the word of a man was the real word. I was still a child, but in the way of work I was already a man."

A Dying City

In 1946, Jerome's City Manager, R.E. Moore, who held the job for twenty-one years, said: "It's more than a little disheartening to see your city going

Cantrell Comix: Ruth Cantrell was a much beloved teacher of art and a member of the Jerome Historical Society. She drew comics of the spooks—the people that stayed behind when the mines closed. Courtesy Jerome Historical Society (2001-083-002).

to pieces in front of your very eyes. … We could rebuild the city … but why should we? There isn't much reason to go to the trouble.

"I guess this is about the only place in America where you can still rent a house or an office or a whole office building, and still keep your shirt and your soul."[18]

Poignant words, but by 1953, an eerie quiet settled into the town. No more explosions. No smoke wafted up from the Clarkdale smelter. No trains and whistles. Not much traffic, especially at night. No birds sang.

The town was dying. Many mourned its loss.

And into that silence came the question, "What now?"

Two
New Beginnings

Speculation ran high in 1953 that the entire town would be razed. A former official of Phelps Dodge Corporation said, "Within a year—grass will grow on the main street of Jerome—Jerome is finished."[19]

It would have been an easy time for the mining companies to bulldoze the rest of the town. There were not a lot of people. Essential services, such as the hospital and schools, had been relocated to the Verde Valley. Phelps Dodge Corporation and Verde Exploration Ltd. owned a great deal of buildings and property in Jerome and beneath it.

The Big Hole Mine

New activity at the open pit, just outside of Jerome, fueled rumors that big scale mining would someday return.

The small mining division of Phelps Dodge leased rights to mine the slopes of the open pit in 1954 to three people that lived in the Verde Valley.[20] They called it The Big Hole Mine and operated it until 1975.[21]

The open pit just outside of the Jerome town limits. When Phelps Dodge closed down big mining, it leased "small mining" rights for The Big Hole Mine. Photo by Bob Swanson, www.SwansonImages.com.

Between eight and twelve men were employed at any given time. They scaled the sides of the pit and drilled into the steep walls and dynamited the ore-bearing rocks. "It was dangerous work," said Robert Sandoval, one of the miners who grew up in Jerome. "The trails were narrow, we were working high up, and the overhangs were large. We'd hide in some of the small caves up there when we blasted."

Miners would separate waste from the ore-bearing rocks, put them in pickup trucks and load them into a railroad car in Clarkdale that was sent weekly to the Phelps Dodge smelter in Douglas, Arizona.

According to Paul Handverger, The Big Hole Mine shipped over 200,000 tons of ore that contained 25 million pounds of copper (12,500 tons), 2,800 ounces of gold, and almost 200,000 ounces of silver.[22]

It was a profitable small business. Mining was discontinued when the surfaces of the open pit could not be further exploited.

Jerome Sets a New Destiny

No one in the town thought Jerome could make a grand comeback, but someone in Clarkdale, the former smelter town for Jerome, did have a vision.

At the Jerome Town Council meeting held on January 30, 1953, Mayor John McMillan called on Jimmie Brewer, a feisty redheaded Scotsman who worked as an administrative officer at Tuzigoot National Monument in Clarkdale.

"Jimmie, you up here to say something?" McMillan asked.

Jimmie: "You people are sitting on your big fat fannies up here on a gold mine and you're not doing a damn thing about it."

McMillan: "Why, what do you mean?"

Jimmie: "I got all these tourists come to the ruins at Tuzigoot and I end up answering more questions about Jerome than about the Indians. They see Jerome sticking up there on the hillside and they want to know about it."

McMillan: "Well, what are we supposed to do about it?"

Jimmie: "Get organized. Get a mine museum going in one of those abandoned buildings. I been dreaming about it for years."

Harry Mader, town clerk and former mayor, asked his secretary to call everyone in Jerome and invite them to a town meeting to discuss the possibility of a museum. On the following Sunday, some thirty-five people showed up, a third of the adult residents. They recognized a lifeline and grabbed hold. They were survivors that were bound together on this small island of a town. If they were going to live here, maybe they had some obligation and responsibility to rescue what was left of it.

Said McMillan, "Some of us held meetings every night for a long many months to start organizing a museum. We started putting the town together again."[23]

Ordinary people seized the opportunity to set a new destiny for themselves that would give Jerome new life. They conjured up ideas for its future and knit themselves together in a common goal. In this way, the community transitioned from city life to village life.

Jerome Historical Society: Our Past is Our Future

In March of 1953, a formal meeting was held to form a historical society. They voted for an Executive Board and officers and defined their mission.[24]

The officers were a solid, honorable, and well-educated group that had grown up in Jerome and Clarkdale. Many of their parents had held jobs working for the mines, school, or hospital, and some in this group had followed in their footsteps. They embraced values of decency, uprightness, and responsibility to themselves, their parents, and their children. Volunteerism was considered a duty and many worked for the town, fire department, school boards, and charitable organizations. The men often wore hats, ties, and polished shoes and boots. Most of the women would not consider being seen in public without makeup and stockings, with hair perfectly in place.

The society opened its bank account with a scant $350: The town of Jerome gave them $200; board member James Haskins donated $50. Within the month, two people bought $100 lifetime memberships. Nonprofit incorporation papers were filed at a cost of $80 on May 7, 1953. Johnie O. Moore and James Haskins were listed as incorporators.

The Jerome Historical Society defined its mission as "to increase and diffuse knowledge of Jerome as a historical and colorful mining city, to maintain a public museum, to protect historic sites and scenic places, to provide facilities for public enjoyment of Jerome's history and scenery, to own, operate, manage, and maintain property, buildings, and facilities." A miner's candlestick was chosen as their emblem. They adopted the motto: "Our Past is Our Future." It was a prophetic vision of the future that came to pass from an investment of less than a thousand dollars.

A Mine Museum Opens on Main Street

Society members decided that the Fashion building on Main Street was in the best shape and would lend itself most economically to the installation of a museum.[25]

It had four floors and a floor space of over 18,000 square feet. Verde Exploration offered to rent the building to the society for fifteen dollars a month, but on the condition that it be on a month-to-month basis. It was not its policy to offer leases to anyone except the U.S. Post Office.

The theme of the museum was the history of mining in the area, which included the Indians that mined salt near Camp Verde and the Spanish expeditions led by Hopis to a small mine on Cleopatra Hill.[26] Hopi people gathered *blue rock* (turquoise, azurite, and malachite) from that mine for hundreds of years to use for pigments in their pictographs.

"Miner Pushing Ore Cart" by William D. White. This painting was the poster cover for the Images of Jerome exhibition in 1999. The painting was part of a series commissioned by Phelps Dodge Corporation in the mid-1930s depicting copper miners. After the Jerome Historical Society formed in 1953, The American Legion loaned six of White's paintings to the society and they were eventually accessioned by the society. Courtesy Jerome Historical Society (A-85-009-003).

Historical society members scoured the mines and found signage, fuse transport boxes, drills, steel-toed safety shoes, lanterns, ore carts, and ore samples to put in the museum. Their big score was the furnace that was used to burn coke in the first mine in the 1870s. It became part of an outdoor display that still exists across the street from the Mine Museum. The Tuzigoot National Monument gave the society some Indian artifacts. Alexander Moisa from The American Legion loaned six oil paintings by William D. White, which were later gifted to the society. The paintings, which were commissioned by Phelps Dodge, depicted miners at their jobs.

RIZONA INDIANS MINED TURQUOISE.
GIL_ITE, AZURITE AND COPPER ORE.
DR_ BOUT INDIAN MINES REACHED
_H CONQUISTADORES AND
E TO THE JEROME AREA IN
37 YEARS BEFORE THE PILGRIMS
ON PLYMOUTH ROCK.

John McMillan, mayor of Jerome and founding member of the Executive Board of the Jerome Historical Society, readies sign for the newly opened Mine Museum. Courtesy Jerome Historical Society (P-1990-102-101).

The Mine Museum opened in mid-May. It had a curio shop and a museum in the back. Volunteers cleaned up the building, with the exception of ten dollars paid to one of the residents to paint the museum and seventy-five dollars for paint. The society voted to pay Leo Sullivan $250 a month to manage the museum.

The society reported at its June 1st meeting that during the first seventeen days that the museum was open, 954 visitors paid twenty-five cents each for a total of $238.50 and bought $441.48 worth of curios.

Nobody foresaw, from that modest beginning, just how powerful and wealthy the Jerome Historical Society would become and what a definitive role it would play in the town's renaissance.

The Ghost of John McMillan

John McMillan was engaged in the twin businesses of life and death after 1953. As town mayor and Executive Board member of Jerome Historical Society, he exerted extraordinary effort to promote Jerome as a tourist attraction; and he operated his family's mortuary business.

John McMillan's father, George, started the mortuary business in 1921. Before then, he worked as a railroad engineer for United Exploration. George asked John to consider joining him in the mortuary business sometime in the 1940s, a career John had never considered.

The story John told about how he learned to be a mortician says a great deal about the middle-class decency and filial duty that was represented by so many people of his generation.

"My dad said, 'You'd better go right on out to the coast, leave the family here, and enter embalming school out there'... It was one of the hardest things I've ever done in my life. I'd been out of school for fifteen or twenty years and then jumped into a school that gave cram courses in pathology, bacteriology, chemistry... that were as foreign to me as anything could be. But I made up my mind, I had three girls in high school, and I thought I'd better set a good example. If I blow this what'll they do? So I made up my mind I was going to learn ... I went home from school every evening with headaches from concentrating 'cause I hadn't really been doing anything like that, but as time moved on, things came easier and it was not long until I was really enjoying it. I got so interested in pathology and bacteriology and medicine, I felt like I would like to have gone on and become a doctor if I'd had the means 'cause it really appealed to me.

"As it turned out I passed the California Board of Embalming and Funeral Directors [exam], which I took right after school, and I came back to Arizona [and passed] the one from the Arizona Board and I might say I was the high man in the Arizona

Board test … I went right into the business with Dad. If we got a death call, we would go and make the call and bring the remains in and I would embalm them.

"I might say that there's a lot of satisfaction in the funeral business, taking care of people. You know, the loss of a loved one to a family, it doesn't happen too often and people are not used to it and they require a lot of help and sympathy and that sort of thing. When you do a good job, they show their appreciation and you feel that it's worthwhile and that was the satisfaction I used to get out of it. Toward the end, Dad got too old and then I lost him and I was alone.

"As for my guiding principles, I feel that a person that strives to do the right thing and is fairly decent about it has a more satisfactory life than oh, these people that are always claiming they can't find themselves and they're trying to find themselves, I don't know what they lost exactly … I've had a good life here and I've raised three nice kids. I think they got a good start here. I really feel that a small town is a good place if it's made of fairly decent citizens."[27]

Three
The Ghost City That Never Existed

Jerome Historical Society members spent their evenings in 1953 gathered in the "Salt Mine," their term for the saloon that had been located in the basement of the new Mine Museum. They churned out signs and brochures. They joked among themselves that they were a bunch of spooks. Once the word "spooks" was mentioned, the members jumped on it as part of the theme for promoting Jerome.

They adopted Luke the Spook as their mascot. Luke was the mythical pixie that World War II soldiers adopted to watch over them in the battlefield.[28]

Society members made new signage. The letters were white on a black background: "Spook's Crossing" on Main Street across from the Mine Museum and "Luke the Spook." They wrapped themselves in sheets and were photographed with the signs. The photographs appeared in newspapers and brochures.

Hand-routed signs, with the same black-and-white motif, were placed on museum exhibits.[29]

Even kids helped out. "Mrs. Cantrell, the art teacher in Clarkdale, taught me how to help carve the signage," said Robert Sandoval, one of the children that lived in Mexican town. "I helped make the sign for the fire station."

At the August 1953 meeting, society members discussed plans for an annual event. They gave it an official name: "Annual Spooks Homecoming, Potluck, and Dance" and invited present and former Jerome families. The event was held in the Salt Mine and was free.

The second Spook Night was held in Lawrence Hall (previously the J.C. Penney store), which the society purchased in 1954. The old wooden floor was a wreck and members worked many nights to make new flooring and nail it down. Some of the kids helped strip the old wood. The building became affectionately known as Spook Hall. Although faded, the J.C. Penney sign still remains. Today the hall is officially named the Richard Lawrence Memorial Hall, in memory of Jerome's postmaster and first member of the society's Executive Board.

"Spooks" on Main Street. Courtesy Jerome Historical Society (HVY-09-21).

The ladies of the society prepared dinner and sold 473 tickets. The party cleared thirty dollars. After the event, the headline from *The Verde Independent* newspaper read: "It was a Hot Night and They Durned Near Tore the Old Town to Pieces."

The Invention of a Ghost City

One evening, some society member, nobody remembers who, dreamed up a sign that cemented the words "Jerome" and "ghost city" in visitors' minds. The sign dramatized Jerome's dwindling population in a sequence of descending numbers, each with a line crossed through it: 15,000, 10,000, 5,000, 1,000. At the end of the sequence were the words, "GHOST CITY."

Two signs were made and society members placed one on the hogback road that led out of town and one at the top of town. From either direction, the town looked desolate. The signs were photographed and sent out with a press release that proclaimed Jerome as "America's First Ghost City." Hundreds of newspapers and magazines picked up the story. Postcards of the image were sold in the Mine Museum.

Historical society members that had never worked in an advertising agency had accomplished the most difficult marketing task of all. They branded Jerome as a ghost city. Magazine and newspaper writers loved the

The "infamous" ghost city sign. Courtesy Jerome Historical Society (HVY-12-17).

ghost town moniker and readers of their articles never saw the name of the town without it.

Tourists told Mine Museum personnel for decades after that they had come to Jerome because of that story. They took photographs of each other next to the signs. The signs disappeared sometime during the 1970s.

A surprising number of visitors navigated the scary highway curves to visit the ghost city and the society's Mine Museum. In the first seven months of operation, 24,401 people wrote their names in the visitor books and 13,116 paid a quarter to view the exhibit and bought curios and postcards. Some signed up as members. By December 31, 1953, the society had five life members that had paid one hundred dollars each and ninety-six active members.

Thus, the history of a wealthy mining Mecca became intertwined with the mythology of a ghost city that never really existed.

A Ghost City Ripe for Pickings

Unfortunately, the promotion of Jerome as a ghost city was an open invitation for vandalism and souvenir hunting from visitors. You could not exactly blame them. The town resembled an immense junkyard in some neighborhoods.

When visitors ventured uptown, they passed the boarded up Methodist Church and the Hotel Jerome, the weedy lots near the concrete ruins of the sliding jail, and rubble on the sides of the roads that was leftover of the big landslide of 1937. On Main Street, the windows of the Boyd and Sullivan Hotels were covered with boards; the Bartlett Hotel had collapsed to walls with no roof; the United Verde Apartments were covered with ivy. Visitors had to watch their feet as they walked on the buckled and cracked sidewalks to go to the Mine Museum, bars, art galleries, or post office—hardly a shopper's paradise. Unless they walked or drove the steep cobblestone streets into some of the neighborhoods, they would not guess that some two hundred and twenty adults and children still lived in Jerome and that some houses were pleasant to live in.

A genuine ghost. Courtesy Ellen Jo Roberts.

Articles about the ghost city, with photographs that displayed its deserted and ramshackle aspects, contained few words about the people that lived in Jerome. How were tourists to know that the ghost city was more of a promotional idea than a reality? How do you invite tourists to a ghost city and then tell them not to take it away?

The kids in Jerome had the run of the town. Billy Watt was quite young when his parents and their two partners bought the Connor Hotel in 1963 and operated the Spirit Room bar downstairs. "My friends and I went into many houses. The beds were made, there was food in the pantry and some of the tables were set. It was kind of spooky and we were afraid to take anything. We also went into the houses at the 500-level. At one point, my parents offered to buy them from Phelps Dodge. It seemed like only weeks after they had asked that Phelps Dodge came in and gutted them."[30]

Jerome's citizens and members of the historical society began to voice concerns as early as 1956 about how the society might have a "tiger by the tail." Bit by little bit, pieces of homes began to disappear. Dick Lawrence, postmaster, newly elected president of the society, and owner of the "Ghost Press," wrote about the downside of the ghost town image in the society's "News Bulletin."[31]

> There was no one act in itself very serious BUT day by day—week by week—month by month we reach a point where practically every vacant house in town is standing wide open. Houses that the absent owners believe to be locked up and secured as they left them. Some of these houses had odds and ends of furniture in them, some were left with considerable stock of personal possession ... WE HAVE A PROBLEM, which possibly does not exist anywhere else in the country ... We do not want to post KEEP OUT and NO TRESPASSING signs all over town. We want our tourist guests to feel free to wander, photograph, paint, and enjoy our GHOST CITY, but still we must insist that they respect the property rights of others without having armed guards patrolling the streets.
> To this end, your society has approved the printing of a little explanatory paper entitled FOR YOUR INFORMATION which the volunteer print shop is turning out in quantity and will be distributed in the form of a "take one" in the Museum lobby ... We are indebted to the city employees to a great extent for the protection they have attempted to give much of this property in the past three years. However it is a never-ending job. Time and material available, houses have been nailed up and boarded up as often as found, but the "nailing up crew" is so badly outnumbered by the other actions that at times they seem to be waging a losing battle. ... If it weren't for vigilant neighbors, woe to the poor widow who had to leave home for a day to visit the doctor or some other imperative business. The fact that fresh laundered curtains are on the windows or a row of well-tended potted plants line the porch or perhaps a few articles of clothing are drying on the breeze doesn't soak through to these people that someone lives here.

What was especially sad was that many people that had lived in Jerome had moved to other jobs but fully expected to return. They locked their homes and left them virtually intact.

Dave Hall, a potter that moved to Jerome in 1970, told me this story. "Soon after I moved to Jerome, I met the son of the Mexican family that had lived next door. He told me that when his parents left Jerome in the early fifties, they boarded up the house and left all their furnishings and housewares so they could just return one day, but they never did. When the son came back to visit the home he grew up in, it was completely emptied out. He was devastated. The house fell completely down in the eighties and you can still see its leftovers of wood and rock walls between the stick poles of Paradise trees."

Tourists were not the only culprits. Many Jeromans that moved here in the 1960s and 1970s told me they carted off windows, doors, bathtubs, toilets, and hardware from houses that were little more than falling-down shacks to help restore ones they rented or bought.

Vandalism plagued Jerome until well into the 1980s, despite efforts at signage and building security. People broke into houses and stole whatever they found. Tourists would wander into obviously restored homes or yards and when caught, they would blandly say, "Oh, we thought Jerome was a ghost city."

The empty streets and Flatiron building on Main Street in the 1950s and '60s. Courtesy Jerome Historical Society (2003-076-003).

John Figi: The Dutchman's Palace

Here is Katie Lee's reminiscence about her friend, John Figi, who moved to Jerome in the 1950s. The story is from a longer piece called "The Dutchman's Palace" published in The Journal of Arizona History *in 2013, used with her permission.*

I met John Figi in a grove of wild Ailanthus, beside a cracked, yet sturdy, old cement building that once was a garage and later a burro stable. Now and then, a few of the town's artists would gather beneath the swishing fronds to visit with the Dutchman. We sat around an old dining room table that was encircled by chairs and screens and parts of wooden fences along with plants and vines potted in various types of mine junk. Water hoses lay coiled at our feet and a 1950s Caddy, on blocks, held down the south corner. It was a restful place that invited conversation.

John was a mischievous man when I met him in 1972—a small, slender, and handsome Hollander of white mane, tanned complexion, theatrical hands, and a voice that once projected from the stage. There was a flow of energy and determination that made sturdy knots in his character. He was a man of infinite patience and varied talents.

I was served iced tea with *poffertjes*, a traditional Dutch pancake ("poffers" for short), along with a steady flow of revelations about his near-to-become-famous Poffer Tent (as it was called in the old country), but when opened to the public would most likely be a "Victorian Poffer Palace."

"I can use ten thousands words and say nothing," he laughs—a self-accusation that never proved out.

He had assembled, reassembled, revised, and restored his workable palace for twenty years to sell it intact to whoever had the money and the desire to operate an authentic poffer kitchen in the same manner that the carnival people of Europe operated them for centuries.

"The price includes me, if they like—I *vill* go *vid* it; to show them how it is done; to provide them with the recipes; and keep them from burning their fingers."

I lived in Jerome for a year before I learned of John Figi's existence, and two years before I heard of the Poffer Palace. It had never been shown publicly and only friends, potential buyers, and antique nuts enjoyed the privilege of his "two-bitless" tour. My first curiosity on the day I was to see it for the first time was, "Where has he hidden it ... if it's of such magnitude as to take twenty years to put together."

John Figi was among the early bohemians to settle in Jerome in the 1950s. Courtesy Jerome Historical Society (JHS2000-54-265).

"One thing you learn in Jerome is that time is an invention," he stated as he guided me toward the front of his cracked, turn-buckled building. "I have been buying, selling, and restoring antiques for well over fifty years, starting at fifteen when I lived in Java with my parents, and I have learned that to be in a hurry is to lose money."

When did you first come to Jerome?

"It was '56, '57—I first saw it on a *droolie* March morning on my way to Sedona with friends. I got out of the car and said, 'Ah, what I couldn't do with this town!'—because you know it looked just like the poor part of the French Riviera; so I thought I might do some restoration on the town if I went into business here, otherwise the people weren't interested in anything but—*when are you leaving?*"

John unlocked the weather-beaten door that I passed each day on my bicycle as

I rode my way up to the post office. Gunnysacks and ancient rotting lace hung in the dirty, streaked windows that fronted the street. The sun's glare was intense against the yellowed stucco building, but as he pushed open the door, sleigh bills tinkled our entrance to a room in a cool, tomb-like darkness. My retinas adjusted slowly, like lights coming up on a stage.

I had stepped into a dreamland!

To say the Poffer Palace was ornate was to understate. It was ingenious, artistically designed and practical. Brass and copper chandeliers with mirrors, the like of which cannot be seen anywhere else—because they were John's put-togethers—hung from the ceiling. Many lights from candelabras, brass lanterns, and the chandeliers glowed softly and outlined carved designs in brass and bronze, and were mirrored in the polished surfaces of seventeenth-century pots. Antique tile, wood, iron, and silver shone through hours of rubbing. The showcase cooking took place in the center ring, for all to see.

The Poffer Palace rebuilt by John Figi. Left to right foreground: Olie Ball container, batter pot, poffer griddle. Background left to right: Waffle oven with food warmer, wall oven and warmer, pump, hutch. Courtesy Katie Lee.

An elaborately turned wooden balustrade enclosed the poffer griddle, sugaring table and basin, warmer and waffle oven. There was a reconstructed Delft tile stove. Outside the enclosure were finely finished rectangular tables with comfortable Douglas chairs where customers sat to eat the delicacies of the house. Mirrors in every sort of ornate wood, brass, and gilded frame lined the walls.

The effect was staggering. After a few minutes of letting it all sink in, John began to explain where it all came from.

"Ornateness has been maintained in the present assemblage because it is a signature of the carnival people who used to be gypsies that came from India seven hundred years ago. From India, they went to Egypt, where they split—one group going through Greece and the Balkans to become the Romanoff gypsies—the others going to Spain. But if I were to call the Visscher family, from whom I bought this stuff in Holland, gypsies, they'd throw me out of the house, because they've been Dutch Reform for over two hundred years. I might add that, in Holland, when ladies put their heads together and say of another woman passing by who is overdressed, 'Vot do you think of *that* getup,' there is always a kind soul who will offer, 'Vell, if you ask me, she looks like a Poffer Tent!'"

I wanted to know why it was called a tent. Surely, all that luxury would not be under a canvas.

"Oh, yes. The gypsies traveled with carnivals, moving from town to town in wagons or flat-bottom boats along the rivers and canals. They were very popular eating places and only served three items—poffers [*pofferjies* in Dutch], waffles, and *olie* balls, a doughnut with a hole. You either bought what they had or were free to leave."

I asked if the same things would be served by the new owners.

"I would hope so, but they can sell fish sticks and hire topless waitresses for all I care—just so long as I get the money. I've reconstructed this Delft tile stove for that very eventuality. They were never in poffer tents. They were built in the walk-in fireplaces of seventeenth-century Dutch homes, where an open fire would be on the hearth with a copper kettle hanging over it. But it has now been converted to a modern gas stove for short-order cooking—keeping the American tastes and public in mind. In fact, what I have done for this poffer tent is very similar to what Mr. Cecil de Mille did for the scriptures—I've glamorized it."

The poffer griddle was supreme in design and usefulness over the many eye-catchers in the center ring. Originally, poffers were made over coal-fired griddles, but John's 1860 griddle was completely modernized with automatic gas burners. Its copper griddle top had sixteen indentations about the size of egg coddlers, each indentation made one little poffer, an inch and a half thick in the middle."

The great waffle oven looked as if it had a fire going in it because John had rigged it with lights and stage gelatins. It stood center at the back of the display in the most prominent spot in the room.

"When I bought it, in the small river town of Dordrecht, it was beautifully painted—black!—over that, thick aluminum paint, and over that, some other hideous stuff, which always gives me a pain where I *neffer* had a headache, because it takes me weeks to get down to the original finish. I've seen the original India ink drawings and it was made in 1859, and the chimney in about 1750.

The part of the poffer griddle that faced the customer and the sugaring table were the most ornate. The filigree and carved brass on these pieces outshone everything but the large copper water boiler that came from Hilversum, Holland. It had a story connected with it that most antique nuts would surely marvel at: "When I found the boiler it had no spigot. Sometime later (in the small village of Steyl, in the province of Limburg, 150 miles from Hilversum) I was on a buying spree—hunting for junk as I call it. In a small shop, hanging from a rope in a dusty corner, were some old brass spigots. 'Oh, you *wouldn't vant* them,' the shopkeeper explained. 'Why not?' I asked. 'Too expensive!'

"I buy cheap, I can tell you," John confided to me with a laugh. "So, I went on to other things, but somehow one of those spigots seemed familiar. Finally, I asked the man if he would take them down, 'How much for this one?' 'That's the most expensive of all. That's seven guilders' (about three dollars). When I got it home, the handmade threads fit perfectly in the boiler. It was the original spigot!"

He lead me to a back corner where the copper and brass coffee urn stood, one with two beautiful porcelain tops to contain coffee and chocolate. He shared a fantasy about the future of the Poffer Palace. "This is where the coffee will be served, piped from modern urns behind, and the waitresses, dressed in their beautiful costumes will get the coffee from the spigot," he demonstrated, and with a little bow, handed me an empty cup, "while the tourists stand around with their cameras taking pictures."

I sat down at one of the tables. It was easy to visualize the Dutchman's Palace in operation.

"I've had a grand time fixing it up. I've met a lot of interesting people, both crooks and crazies; still I will be happy to see it operating again in a proper setting, if not here, some other likely place."

I said, "You've got it all figured out, haven't you, John?"

"Oh, yes, of course. This is show business, you know!"

Coda

In the 1970s and 1980s, Katie was a musician-writer-performer who traveled much of the time. On one of her return trips, she was introduced to a woman who was going to purchase, or had purchased, the Poffer Palace. "I remember she was dressed like a Californian, and I did not trust much of what she was saying—about how-when-where she was going to open the Poffer Palace—even after going through it one more time with her as she pointed out various things that were her favorites.

"When I came back to Jerome in March of 1979 or 1980, John had gone ... the building empty ... nothing in the patio ... only the cracked cement and Ailanthus trees. I asked my friend Richard Martin if he knew what happened."

"John went back to Holland, y'know."

"Does anyone know where that woman he sold it to opened the Poffer Palace?" I asked.

"We've heard that she's selling it off piecemeal ... it's worth plenty. She's just an antique dealer, that's all ... wouldn't know how to fry an egg, probably, let alone open and run John's Poffer Palace. I always thought it would look great outside here ... under a tent ... among these trees."

Four
The Jerome Historical Society Becomes a Large Property Owner

The demolition of the T.F. Miller commissary, the Con O'Keefe building, and the Ewing Transfer building in 1953 left large visual holes and a big rubble pile on Main Street. Their destruction was a gloomy reminder of the prophecy that uptown Jerome would soon turn to grass and served as a wake-up call for the newly established Jerome Historical Society.

During the society's December 5th, 1953, meeting, "Mr. McMillan moved that the secretary write Verde Exploration Limited and the Phelps Dodge Corporation asking that we be given a chance to discuss the sale of any building that may be put up for sale in Jerome. We don't want to remove them, but will assume taxation and liability for any damage."[32] The society also appointed a committee to investigate acquiring other buildings in Jerome.

The Jerome Historical Society Buys Property

In February 1954, Clarence J. Beale, Verde Exploration's manager in Jerome and a society board member, wrote to the New York Board of Verde Exploration asking if they would be willing to sell the Mine Museum building. Verde Ex offered to sell it at the salvage price of $150 plus $75 for the lot on which the building stood. They offered to apply the society's paid-up rentals as payment for the lot.

The society learned in May of 1954 that Christ Church (the Episcopal church) was up for sale. They voted to write to the bishop of the diocese in Phoenix. The diocese agreed to sell the building for $170.

Society board member John McMillan had a particular interest in the church because his father, George, laid its cornerstone in 1927. George was Grand Master of the Grand Lodge of Arizona Masons at the time. McMillan said that it was a "great and rare honor for a grand master to be presented with laying the church cornerstone in his own community."[33]

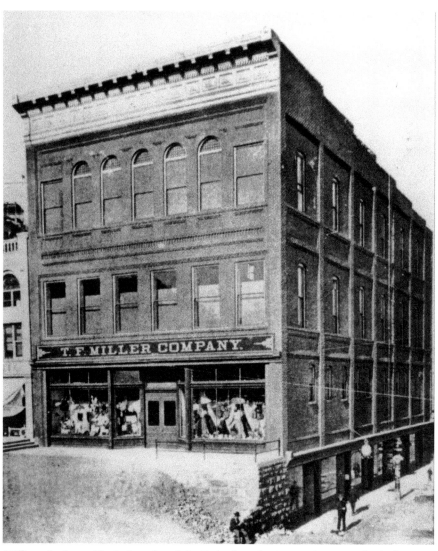

William Andrews Clark, founder of the United Verde Copper Company, built the T.F. Miller building in 1899 at a cost of $100,000, a grand price in those days. The mine's official commissary, the lifeblood of the mining community, held sentinel at the center of town on Main Street just opposite the Connor Hotel. It was demolished in 1953 and a large rubble pile was left behind. Courtesy Jerome Historical Society (rj-90-285).

The society purchased the J.C. Penney building (Spook Hall) from the Dicus family in June of 1954 for $1,000. Dr. Arthur Brant, a geophysicist who worked in Jerome for Newmont Exploration Company, loaned the society $500.

The society took giant steps to become the stewards of Main Street buildings.[34]

Board members, welded together by a single goal, worked to make signs, do repairs, and promote the town. It was community building on a scale they hardly imagined when they began the society. Love of the town and its history, not money or power, propelled their dreams forward, in those days.

Ten Dollar Sale of Main Street Properties

Verde Exploration (Verde Ex) sold ninety parcels of land and buildings to the Jerome Historical Society in June 1956 for a total of ten dollars—but only to a depth of twenty-five feet.[35]

The deed included the same parcels the mining company purchased in the late 1930s to avoid lawsuits from the 1937 landslide that wiped out three blocks of Jerome. The deed included all the buildings on the block that held the New State Motor building, which contained the U.S. Post Office (except for the privately owned Connor Hotel), the next block of buildings that included Paul's Place, the abandoned shop next to it, and the shell of the Bartlett Hotel. The society also took ownership of the buildings across the street, including the Pay'n Takit Safeway Grocery, the Boyd Hotel, the Sullivan Apartments, the Starr building, and half of the building that now houses the Cactus Shop. The deed also included the sliding jail and a number of empty lots on Main Street and the streets below. The buildings needed a lot of stabilization and repair before they could be occupied.

The deed contained language that forbade the society to sue Verde Ex or Phelps Dodge Corporation for any damage or injury caused, "directly or indirectly, by the subsidence, disturbance, slippage or other movements, of or injury to, the surface or other part of the premises hereby conveys, or any improvements thereon, on account of mining or other operations."[36]

Clarence J. Beale, a society board member and employee of Verde Ex, was instrumental in convincing the mining company to give the property to the society, according to geologist Paul Handverger.[37]

The stewardship of the society toward its buildings cemented a positive relationship between the society and Verde Ex. Both wanted to protect the town from further collapse.

This purchase gave the society immediate income from rents from the post office and Paul's Place.

The rubble that was the sliding jail, etc., after the slide of 1937. Courtesy Jerome Historical Society (J-90-439-33).

View of Jerome from the cemetery outside of town. Photo by Art Clark from Ballad of Laughing Mountain. *Courtesy Jerome Historical Society (2003-076-001).*

The August 1957 "News Bulletin" of the society was jubilant:

FIRST we are glad, and we know that you will be too, to be able to
report that no more buildings will be torn down in the main part of
GHOST CITY. The successful conclusion of negotiations started in
December 1953 has resulted in the greater part of "uptown" Jerome
being purchased by and turned over to the Society ... We now hold title
to most of the remaining property on Main Street, except that which is
privately owned, and also enough vacant lots to build another city if the
darned things would ever stop moving. Too late to save such landmarks
as the Bartlett Hotel and the Shea building, we are dedicated to preserving what remains ... A carefully planned gradual restoration of some
of this property will net your Society additional usable rental property
which will ensure a steady income and furnish capital."

That purchase would eventually make the Jerome Historical Society
one of the wealthiest historical societies in Arizona. It also shifted a great
deal of the business of the society into property management. This included
repair, rentals, and payment of taxes and insurance.

The Downside of Being a Large Property Owner

The society's jubilance turned to distress when it received a large tax bill
for its properties from the county assessors in 1958. The bill came close
to putting the society "on the rocks." Because the society was renting out
property, their nonprofit tax-exempt status was also challenged. The society's "News Bulletin" sounded the alarm.

Even completely ignoring the possibility of a tax problem, which we did
not then know existed, we were well aware that the liabilities in assuming
ownership of so many run-down and neglected buildings were going to
be equal or in excess of any income we would receive from all of them.
However, when the first year's tax bill gobbled up ALL of the rental
income and beat our "other receipts" bank balance down to a few bucks
(less than enough to pay our light and water bills), much less "operate," it
became apparent that IF your Society was going to continue to exist, we
were going to have to do SOMETHING.

After quite a few discussions, which included ideas such as disposing all
of its rental properties and converting the rental properties into a holding
company, the society decided to try negotiating with the county officials

for tax rates more compatible with real values and a way to continue to use rentals to restore the property without affecting their tax-exempt status. One of their arguments was that the assessments were unrealistic given the run-down condition of the buildings and the fact that sales of business properties were unlikely. They used the example of the Episcopal Church, which was assessed at $3,000. A mudslide slammed into it, which all but wrecked the back of the building. It was worth perhaps little more than the $170 that the society paid for it.

The society's negotiation was successful. The county assessors lowered the property taxes, which helped keep the society financially stable. New rental clients would have to be found, however, not easy for a town that was advertising itself as a ghost city. The only newcomer renting space were the artists Shan and Roger Holt who founded the Verde Valley Artists a few months after the society was incorporated.

Property management became a monumental job for historical society volunteers.

Five
The 1960s: Jerome is Feted for Its History

Two major events leveraged Jerome's reputation as a mining history destination—the opening of the Jerome State Historic Park and the town's designation as a National Historic Landmark. The events feted Jerome's history, but brought in very little new income.

No new businesses offered to rent space from the Jerome Historical Society. Annual visitation averaged 30,000 during the decade and yearly income fluctuated between $16,000 and $20,000. About a fourth of that income was from tourists. Annual rents brought in $2,600. Income from museum sales was offset by inventory purchases and salary for the museum manager. Most of the rest of the society's income went to the repair of its buildings, with priority given to the museum and maintenance of their rental properties.

Maybe two-dozen people moved out and about the same number moved in. A few newcomers were artists; others had jobs or businesses that were not dependent on Jerome for income. Earl Bell, a distinguished laser scientist, moved to Jerome and bought the mining executives' homes and the Little Daisy Hotel, which were built by United Verde Extension. The Connor Hotel/Spirit Room building changed hands, and new owners John and Faye Watt began the job of restoration. Their son Billy Watt remembered that the ceiling of one of the rooms collapsed and five hundred wheelbarrows of dirt and debris had to be hauled out. The Candy Kitchen restaurant changed hands. A few new businesses opened: a restaurant called the House of Joy that was open only

Gold mine with the Little Daisy Hotel in the background. Photo by Bob Swanson, www.SwansonImages.com.

on weekends, one antique store, and an Indian curio shop. The uptown grocery store was still open.

The historical society gave part of the upper park, the lower park, the sliding jail and some of the lots in the slide area to the town of Jerome, properties it could ill afford to keep up and pay taxes. In the town's boomtown years, these properties would become valuable parking areas. At the time, however, the town could barely pay its bills, much less keep up with repairs to the water, sewer, and drainage systems, which showed signs of major deterioration.

Mudslides and erosion destroyed much of the drainage system on Cleopatra Hill, which caused damage to the buildings below. Mayor John McMillan decided to try a novel fix. He paid a few local boys to gather *Ailanthus altissima* (tree of heaven or Paradise tree) seeds and fill three large canvas bags with them. McMillan flew his Aeronica Chief single-engine plane over Jerome and dumped the seeds, like an airborne "Johnny Appleseed." He hoped they would take hold on Cleopatra Mountain, but instead, they landed in Jerome's gullies and washes, and left the mountain still bare. Jerome grew such a thick patch of Paradise trees within the next twenty years that roots ripped down walls and clogged sewer and water pipes.

The town was so quiet, still so devoid of traffic, that several people told me of concerts held in the street outside of Shorty Powell's house on Hull Avenue, just below Main Street. Shorty was one of the artists that had moved to Jerome in the late fifties. Lawn chairs would be set out in the middle of the street and he'd put classical music and jazz records on his turntable and turn the volume up.

The population of Jerome was 243 people, according to the 1960 census, and it did not change much during that decade. Many loved the peacefulness of neighborhood life.

The Ghosts of the Tamale Ladies

Aurelia Gonzales, born in 1898, moved to Jerome in 1921 with her husband, Felipe Islas, from a small mountain town in the province of Jalisco, Mexico. She was twenty-three and he was a dashing revolutionary who had ridden with Pancho Villa and found a job in one of the Jerome mines. Islas died in 1931 and Aurelia married Jose Fernando Gonzales, who worked for the United Verde Extension mine. She found a job as Jimmy Douglas' personal laundress. They had no children.

Santos Contreras, Aurelia's widowed sister, moved to Jerome in 1944 to live with her. Santos was forty-nine years old and had seven children.

Aurelia and Santos made tortillas and tamales on a wood stove. Twice a day, they walked the mile and a half from their home just past the high school up to the main part of town to sell them to restaurants and grocery stores. When the stores closed, Aurelia and Santos sold their products directly to the people. Over time, they affectionately became known as "The Tamale Ladies."

Diane Geoghegan, an artist who moved to Jerome in the 1970s, befriended Aurelia and Santos. Diane rented a small house from them near the cemetery. "Although they lived a life of poverty by today's standards, they kept a clean house, grew their own corn, vegetables, and herbs, kept chickens for food and birds for eggs. If you went

"Aurelia Gonzales and Santos Contreras, known affectionately as the tamale ladies, were among the only people that I knew that lived the same life in the same house in virtually the same circumstances throughout the different incarnations of Jerome. Both celebrated hundred-year birthdays in Jerome."
—Artist Diane Geoghegan. Photo by ML Lincoln.

to their home, there would always be beans and coffee, stories, and the hospitality that is so warmly and openly extended to friends and family. I hope that anyone who wants to enrich their own life will seek out and help the older people in our communities. 'Living legends' have a lot to offer."[38]

The Douglas Mansion Becomes a State Park

When Jimmy Stuart Douglas' mine, the United Verde Extension, struck it rich in 1915, he built a beautiful white mansion for his family. It featured a wine cellar, billiard room, marble shower, steam heat, and, much ahead of its time, a central vacuum system.[39]

Douglas Mansion engulfed in clouds at sunrise. Photo by Ron Chilston.

It had panoramic views of the Verde Valley, the canyons and ramparts of the Mogollon Rim, and the San Francisco peaks that towered above Flagstaff. Equally spectacular were the views of the town of Jerome and the United Verde mine.

When the mine closed, the mansion was boarded up and locked. It remained virtually deserted until the Douglas family put it on the market in the late 1950s for $40,000. As there were no takers, the family soon lowered the price to $10,000. Even so, they were unable to sell it.[40]

The Douglas family donated the mansion and 2.43 acres of land to the State of Arizona as a state park museum in 1962.

The Jerome State Historic Park was dedicated and opened to the public as Arizona's fifth state park on October 16, 1965. Its official designation was the Douglas Memorial Mining Museum.

It was dedicated to the history of the Douglas family and the United Verde

Douglas Mansion (Jerome State Park) with mining shaft in front yard in the mid-1980s. Photo by Bob Swanson, www.SwansonImages.com.

Extension Mine. Guests were welcomed to the dedication by the newly elected mayor of Jerome and the chairman of the State Parks Board. Lewis Douglas, Jimmy Douglas' son, was an honored guest speaker. Lewis lived in Tucson, Arizona, after an illustrious career as a U.S. congressman and ambassador to the United Kingdom.

Rooms on the first floor had been remodeled for museum displays. Douglas' living room was redesigned with a lowered circular ceiling to accommodate them. The architect worked with sculptor Phillip Sanderson on many of the dioramas, photos, and wall murals. Parking and picnic areas were constructed.

The opening festivities coincided with Jerome's annual "Spook Night" and the celebrations lasted all day and into the night.[41]

The Jerome Historical Society operated the museum's concession stand for many years.

Henry Vincent, CPA and longtime Jerome resident told me, "I have long held the opinion that the Douglas family donated the mansion to prevent the possible condemnation of the town by Phelps Dodge, who contemplated removing the town in order to strip back the overburden to access the rich remaining ore lode. When I was a kid, the old timers told starry-eyed children stories of the untapped riches, which still lay beneath Jerome. I believe that Douglas' transfer of the home to the state park and Jerome's subsequent placement on the National Register would have assisted in preventing a condemnation of the town. I also believe that the Douglas family had the knowledge, power, and family self-interest to oppose a condemnation and to plan for the potential thereof."

Uptown Jerome Becomes a National Historic District

The opening of the new Douglas State Park and efforts by the Jerome Historical Society led to the designation of the commercial district of Jerome as a National Historic District. Stewart L. Udall, United States Secretary of the Interior, came to Jerome on April 19, 1967, to present the historic plaque.

"The Jerome Historic District has been designated a Registered National Historic Landmark under the provision of the Historic Sites Act of August 21, 1935. This site possesses exceptional value in commemorating and illustrating the history of the United States. U.S. Dept. Interior, 1967."

The Verde Independent front-page headline read, "Udall Tells Jerome It Must Preserve Its Proud History." Udall also spoke at the Chamber of Commerce breakfast in Clarkdale. "This type of beauty you in the Verde Valley take for granted is something very special. ... You have demonstrated the tremendous interest people have in the past by what has been done at Jerome. If people are interested today, what will be their attitude fifty years from now? You have something here in Verde Valley which is priceless, and you must care for it. ... In any other state, this area would be a National Park."[42]

In 1976, the town of Jerome was designated as a National Historic Landmark.

The Freak Storm of 1967

A freak winter storm in 1967 came close to wiping out whatever gains had been made in repairing buildings and infrastructure. In mid-December, Jerome was blanketed under four feet of snow. Every street was blocked. Huge drifts almost buried some of the houses. Power was knocked out. The freak storm was unexpected. Daytime temperature in the Verde Valley for the preceding two days had been above 50 degrees. But when two slow-moving winter weather systems collided, they created meteorological history in Arizona.[43]

The back part of Paul and Jerry's Saloon caved in; the roof of the Mine Museum building was damaged; the Phelps Dodge warehouse roof collapsed; a great deal of damage occurred to homes that had been abandoned, particularly on Company Hill. A house fire burned unchecked because fire equipment could not get through the snow-blocked streets. Retaining walls buckled and fell, and drainage systems were damaged during the heavy runoff.

The snowstorm was a financial catastrophe.

But from a kid's point of view, the snowstorm was heaven.

"That was the best time of my life, I'll tell you what!" Billy Watt told me. "I was maybe seven years old. We were stuck for eight days. Nobody could get in or out. Some of the other kids and I would grab trashcan covers from the bar and we'd slide down Main Street over and over and over again. It was a wonderful thing."

Henry Vincent, whose parents moved to Jerome in the 1960s, told me, "My older friends made real good money shoveling roofs. They would tie ropes around their midsections, secure them to the chimneys and shovel. Then they would jump from the roofs onto the huge snow piles."

Paul Handverger, Clarkdale's Civil Defense director reported, "At the end of the fifth day of the storm, the town was still in bad shape. Only one lane was open on Jerome's Main Street and the community was on only three-quarters electricity. … Volunteers brought food and medicine to Jerome residents trapped and isolated in their homes. … One of the colorful personalities living in Jerome since the nineteen-twenties was eighty-nine-year-old Clarence J. Beale, who had worked as a bookkeeper for James 'Rawhide' Douglas of the UVX and was the longtime agent for its successor company, Verde Exploration Ltd., which was my employer at the time. He lived in one of the homes just above the UVX mine yard next to the Miner's Hotel [Little Daisy Hotel] at the end of UVX road.

"During the storm, I called Mr. Beale and asked him how he was doing and did he need anything. His answer caught me off guard as I expected him to list some foods or other necessities since he was isolated and trapped by the snow. All he requested was a large bag of seed for the birds around his home and a bottle of bourbon for him to enjoy while watching the birds feed. I foolishly argued with him that I should bring food, but gave that up after only for a few seconds. Interrupting me, he let me know in his strong voice and salty language that the birdseed and the bourbon were all that he wanted.

"So, during the failing light at the end of the day, I strapped on a pair of borrowed snowshoes from Arizona Public Service. ... That Saturday evening found me parking my four-wheel drive out at 89A and snowshoeing down the UVX Mine Road with a large bag of birdseed and a bottle of bourbon over snowdrifts as deep as twelve feet to Mr. Beale."[44]

A Town in Crisis Management

A report prepared for the Historical Society to make recommendations about how to attract tourism read, "Jerome was still very close to decay, particularly in the business district. Every day finds another wall in the business district a little nearer collapse and another building a little nearer the point of no return ... Piles of rat-infested rubble or empty foundations are not the kind of thing that can be advertised as tourist attractions. Continuation ... can only lead to the final disappearance of 'historic' Jerome."[45]

It was not just the business district that was in trouble. Many homes in Jerome had significant damage and were no longer considered livable. Many areas were firetraps. And because the big buildings that visually dominated Jerome were boarded up, the town looked like a ramshackle ghost town.

It was extremely difficult to bring Jerome out of its recessionary, survival mode. A sustainable source of income and something of a miracle were needed. Fortunately, both occurred, but from wholly unexpected directions that had little to do with tourism or mining history.

The photo of this home was captured just before it collapsed in 1985. Photo by Bob Swanson, www.SwansonImages.com.

Six
The Invasion of the Hippies

Change blew in from an unexpected direction. About 175 cultural and social renegades took up residence in Jerome during the late 1960s and early 1970s. Some were artists, writers, and musicians; some were homosexuals; some could not stand authority of any kind; some were Korean War or Vietnam vets; a few were computer programmers and scientists. Esther Burton, one of Jerome's new residents, put all of them into one category, "The backwash of the avant-garde." I call them hippies in this book because that is how the majority of the people that lived here considered them.[46]

It was also how many of the newcomers referred to each other. They were counterculture people at odds with the established mores. They felt disenfranchised of the principles of nonviolence that they held so dear.

Through a large, informal underground linked by rock 'n' roll, LSD and pot, communal living and free love, Jerome became known as a desirable hippie redoubt, along with San Francisco's Haight Ashbury and Taos, New Mexico. The hippies arrived in their wildly painted VW buses, Plymouth Valiants, and Chevy pickups.

Many were young, and like the town itself, derelicts with many needs. They had yet to figure out their future. They rented dilapidated shacks and rooms in equally dilapidated apartments for as little as fifteen dollars a month and bought homes for under a thousand dollars.

Because Jerome was a hundred miles from any large urban area, a frontier-like, free-for-all atmosphere prevailed. The hippies' appetite for drugs and sex went virtually unchecked. They sprinkled hashish on their scrambled eggs, smoked pot, munched peyote buttons and brownies made with pot, and took copious amounts of LSD. They planted pot in their backyards and makeshift greenhouses. They went to Sycamore Canyon and the Verde River where they dropped their clothes and hung out and philosophized about a future free from assassinations and war and full of peace, love, and brotherhood.

With so much room for improvisation, the hippies began to reinvent their lives. Jerome became their portal of reincarnation; a town of like-minded spirits cherished, protected, and accepted by their peers. They knit themselves into one big, extended, dysfunctional family.

Some of Jerome's hippies sitting on the steps opposite the Spirit Room circa 1982. Courtesy Jerome Historical Society (1995-30-1).

Theirs was a world of enchantment, irreverence, and eccentricity. Out of this rowdy bunch would come many of Jerome's future political leaders, innovators, builders, artists, business owners, and scoundrels.

Arrival Tales

When did you arrive and where did you live was part of most any conversation I had with people that lived in Jerome. These were some of the answers they gave me. Although not everybody called themself a hippie, most of the people they partied with were, so it was sometimes difficult to make distinctions. You will meet the people mentioned below in many of the chapters that follow, as they helped in Jerome's restoration.

Dave Hall, 1970

"My first home in Jerome was the bottom floor of Anne, George, and Nick Laddich's house on East Avenue. I had saved $300 to move here and the rent was $35 a month. Other people who lived on that street were the Dimitrovs, Pecharichs, Selnas, and Vincents. All of them had dogs and all of them barked. I made friends with Mama Laddich, who called me 'boy,' spoke in broken English and brought me borscht and strudels. The Dimitrovs were spooky folks that had a mentally retarded daughter they kept locked up, but sometimes she'd escape and they'd run up and down the street chasing her.

"Living on that street felt old world, very Eastern Europe. I guess I fit in pretty good. I didn't have long hair. I was not totally scary to them like some of the hippies. I was pretty much a hermit who painted and drew. But I did go to the big pool in Sycamore Canyon and swam naked and smoked dope and took LSD with the dozens of other hippies around. To make money, I drove a little route between Prescott and Flagstaff where people paid $10 for my drawings."

Dave cofounded the shop, Made In Jerome Pottery; he became fire chief in 1981.

Mimi and Lew Currier, 1970

"In 1970, Bill and Betty Bland and son Abe, Mimi and I and our son Chris, and another couple from Hawaii moved here as a commune and bought a fifteen room house on seven city lots near the elementary school for $7,000. It was called the "Lyons" house after a couple that had lived here during the mining days. Our friend from Hawaii got stopped in Phoenix for a traffic ticket and when they ran his license plate, they got him on draft evasion and impounded the car. His girlfriend was left sitting on the side of the road and we went down and got her, but she stayed only a few months. One thousand dollars bought us tools from what used to be an industrial wood shop. Bill went to Los Angeles for a few months to learn how to make classical guitars and when he came back, that's what we started doing. We opened up a luthier shop on lower Main Street. It lasted about three years."

Lew was town clerk in the early eighties and was twice elected to serve as a council member for the town of Jerome. Mimi served on many boards, including the Verde Valley Art Association, Jerome Historical Society, and the Jerome Humane Society.

Katie Lee, 1971

"Betty Bell had a gallery uptown and it was her fault I was here. She knew of a house for rent. 'No way I'm going to live on damaged earth. It's a dead town.' 'Yeah,' said Betty, 'but you'll love the price.' I went to see it. Ninety dollars a month was way less than the $250 a month I paid in Sedona. There was black and white linoleum in the front entrance, and one wall was painted the most god-awful purple with green trim. It was the most horrible color combo I'd ever seen. The windows faced down the gulch, which looked like an ugly junk pile. I paid the rent, moved my furniture and plants, put my bags down, and handed the keys to the only two guys I knew and asked them to please water my plants. Then I headed to Princeton, New Jersey, to begin another tour of the United States as a folk singer."

Doyle Vines, 1971

"I was twenty-one years old, disillusioned, grasping for sanity following a nervous breakdown that was triggered by a tragic love affair. Although it was sunny in the valley, as I drove up the road to Jerome, I became encased in a dense fog. The time of year was around Thanksgiving. I made the turn at the Spirit Room and parked. I saw a glow through the fog, crossed the street and walked toward it. I walked into the Spirit Room, which was full of long hairs just like me. Some of the guys were playing pool. Some of the ladies, most in long skirts, were sitting around sewing, knitting, and laughing. There were babies asleep in their snugglies, baskets, and on top of blankets and coats on the benches. Cats and dogs peacefully curled together under the pool table. I walked in from the si-

The Spirit Room became a favorite hangout of the hippies that moved to Jerome. Overheard inside the Spirit Room: "I can't think straight in Jerome—it's like you're on a space ship and you get less and less to feeling like going down or getting off." Photo by Bob Swanson, www.SwansonImages.com.

lence of the fog into abundant life. I fell instantly in love with Jerome. I felt I had found home."

Doyle served as town manager, town clerk, assistant town clerk, city planner, zoning administrator, building inspector and crewman, some concurrently. He moved from Jerome in the late 1980s.

Paul Nonnast, 1972

"When I came to this place for the first time, I got hit in my solar plexus. There was a sense of nostalgia and some latent memory of having seen it before. A poignant déjà vu. I remember standing at the post office and looking up to the warehouse and my solar plexus was yawning open, with no rational reason why, but it seemed a pretty profound response to being here.

"The only car on the street was an old Ford Falcon. The windows were very grey and foggy, like the windows of the church across the street. Newspapers were piled so high that I could see three little yipping dogs running up and down and around like one of those horse carousels you see in carnivals.

"My eyes drifted out to the dirt road leading out of town from the old post office. Two funky miners were coming into town on their burros loaded with panning equipment and rock hammers.

"As I looked down Main Street, a woman with tobacco-colored glasses, wearing a long dress from the thirties, sat statue-like outside a rock shop.

"The only sound was Caruso's operatic tenor blaring from a scratched record. I walked to the corner of the Spirit Room to find it was coming from the English Kitchen. Standing outside was a Chinaman wearing skirt-like white pants, black slippers, stained white restaurant apron, and a white coolie hat.

"The whole scene was as surreal as any hallucination."

Paul became an architect, sculptor, and fine arts painter. He died in 2005.

John and Iris McNerney, 1973

"We bought a house in Jerome for $13,000 in a desolate and empty town. It was all we could afford and the view was astounding. The first winter was brutal, there was one wood stove for four rooms, and no insulation. When the wind blew, the upstairs floor rippled.

"The cast of characters was astounding, old-school bohemians and hordes of hippies that always seemed to be talking about how stoned they were. I had a patent on a mercury detector I couldn't sell, my geology pick, and an old rusty saw. I bought a few tools and set myself up as a furniture maker. In America you can do anything you want to do without the credentials, except maybe law and doctoring. In Europe, there's no way I could have just set myself up as a furniture maker without going through the apprenticeships. That's America. The land of initiative."

John founded Jerome Instrument Corporation in 1978.

Richard Martin, 1973

"I was twenty-seven years old when I left San Diego, sick of my old life and feeling insecure and inadequate about who I was. I needed to sort myself out away from the influences of my family and the city where I had such deep roots. Only by going away did I feel I could get into a different space and figure out my own dreams.

"I didn't know where to go, but I was offered a job in Albuquerque. On the way, I stopped in Jerome, an old ghost town that I had visited as a child. I stopped at the Spirit Room bar and started having so much fun that I got stuck here and stayed.

"During the first three months I camped in a nearby canyon with my new friends Gypsy John, Virgo Bill, and Little John, who was fifteen. We hung out nude, surrounded by sun and red rocks, swimming in the clear pools, smoking dope, doing peyote, reading books, hanging out with girls, and being philosophical.

"Virgo Bill and I found a place in the bottom of the Haskins, which was owned by John Watt, owner of the Spirit Room bar. There was no electricity, no water, no bathroom, no nada. We shit at the bar and peed outside. We were told we could live there as long as there were no women. But then one morning Priscilla the Gypsy Queen walked in with her big hoop earrings and before I knew it, she had taken off her clothes and gotten into my bed. John Watt caught us in the act. Watt kicked me and Virgo Bill out for violating the 'no girls' rule."

Richard was appointed to the Jerome Town Council in 1978. He was elected mayor in 1980 and served two other terms as a council member.

Ron Ballatore, 1977

"I arrived from Long Beach, California, looking for a change. The town looked small, dilapidated, almost deserted and peaceful. I was instantly labeled as a biker with a Mexican wife. The biker part was accurate, but my wife Pam was not Mexican. For sure we weren't hippies, although we began to make some friends in the hippie community. Some of the old-timers, particularly some of the Croats and Serbs, took an instant dislike to us. We found it to be not a friendly town. There was a lot of non-acceptance of newcomers, not just hippies."

Ron was water commissioner, town manager, and chief of police.

The Ghost of the Gun (1970s)

At night, only at night, could Hilde and Jerry, newcomer hippies to Jerome, hear the voice of an old lady croaking from a shack across the wash in the Gulch. "What are you doing in this house; get out of this house; where is Frankie; you forgot the dog food." Hilde and Jerry never saw her, but they knew she was there because every week they would bring a bag of groceries and leave it at the bottom of the steps of her shack. The next morning, the bag was always gone. The strangeness of the place they had moved to sometimes made them shiver.

From time to time, a tap, tap, tapping was heard from the vicinity of the outhouse. Tap. Tap. Tap. It was the sound of the old lady tapping the cardboard latch to shut herself in.

Her family from over by Prescott knew she was still there. From time to time they would pile out of a disheveled Chevy and call and call her, venturing no farther than the bottom of the steps. She stayed silent and never came out. Eventually, they would go away.

When Father John would come with a delegation of neighbors to beg her to come back to church, she would never appear, but would chase them away with loud curses from her witch's mouth.

No one ever saw her.

One day, there was a small grass fire just outside her house. Scott Owens, her next-door neighbor, called the firemen. He grabbed a fine Oaxacan blanket he hoped he would not have to use and his fire extinguisher. He sat on a wall close by as the antique fire engine charged toward the shack.

He watched as the door of the shack opened and the old lady appeared. She was small like a child and he did not see her face. A torn dress hung from her stooped shoulders. She was a frail, crumpled wraith. Slowly and with no apparent rush, she advanced toward the little grass fire with a glass of water in her hands. She threw the water on the fire and watched the flames sputter just slightly before she turned and slowly walked back into the shack. She watered the fire twice more before the firemen arrived and put out the fire with their long hoses. The firemen called to the old lady, but she did not come out.

Scott never saw her again. But at night for quite some years, he would hear the tap, tap, tapping at the outhouse along with the distant yipping of coyotes.

Artists Nancy and Lee Louden bought the shack from the daughter of the old lady sometime in the mid-1970s. The walls were so close they could touch them with their arms barely stretched. The ceiling had caved into a V. They found a rusty twenty-two rifle on the wall and newspaper clippings that revealed that the old lady's son and daughter had a child together and that when it was born, the son killed it with the rifle and fled. They found another clipping that said the son escaped from prison.

The gun holds their ghosts—the confusions of the son, the tears of the daughter, and the anguish of a mother who watched her son become a murderer.

The Hippies: A Mockery of Jerome's Old Way of Life

The hippies were not welcomed with open arms. Most residents, particularly the older ones, felt that they had been invaded by a swarm of smelly drug addicts and no-good thieves. They despised them as a mockery of what they considered the American way of life. It felt like a plague they were ill-prepared to cope with.

"Jerome's decaying shacks have attracted the hippies and other characters with decaying morals. Some of the dangers in Jerome are gradually lessening because citizens are 'getting involved' enough to persuade the shiftless that they are too conspicuous in Jerome anyway."[47]

The house in the Gulch that Richard Martin bought for $375 in 1975 and restored. Photo by Jonathan Tudan, courtesy Richard Martin collection.

Many Mexicans found the hippies' lifestyles unacceptable. Robert Sandoval, who grew up in Jerome, said, "We used to call the hippies freeloaders, because they seemed lazy and would use the system. Most of the homes they lived in didn't have running water and they looked rather unclean, especially the ones with matted hair and dirt under their fingernails. Their free-love movement was not accepted in our communities. I could have been chief of police if I agreed to run them out of town, but I didn't want to do that."

Some people in Jerome were more actively violent. When Channel 10 TV News did a story on a hippie fixing up a house in the Gulch, a few self-appointed vigilantes tore the house down.

The Jerome Town Council ran an active campaign to get rid of them. A common tactic was to sic the building inspector on their houses for unsafe construction, a problem that was ubiquitous throughout Jerome. The town ordered the new building inspector to not issue building permits to hippies. He was also ordered to condemn and tear down houses that hippies had moved into and he entered into talks with a Sedona contractor who would be allowed to salvage what he could. The order caused a furor that galvanized Jerome Historical Society president Peggy Mason to lead a sit-in at one of the buildings that was condemned. It was the first time that non-hippie newcomers organized against the old-timers.[48]

Richard Martin was the first hippie to run for office. He entered the 1976 Town Council election but did not get elected. When somebody resigned from that council, he was not asked to fill in, even though he was sixth in number of votes. "Three reactionary right wingers were in the majority. When they threatened to 'out' a homosexual council member, he resigned and so did a woman named Barbara Hogan, when it was discovered that her husband was having an affair with one of the cops. I was appointed mayor in 1978 and for a while we operated as a council of four members. I was officially elected in 1980 with a big victory," Martin said.

Illegal Search and Seizure Ordinance

The wild Fourth of July party in 1968 mixed hippies with outlaw motorcycle gangs that tore up the town. The gangs smashed windows at Paul and Jerry's Saloon and made themselves generally obnoxious. The Town Council found the incident an excuse to target hippies and, in a special meeting, passed a gun ordinance, which made it legal in Jerome for the police to search anyone that was suspected of carrying weapons. The ordinance drew an immediate letter of protest from a member of the National Rifle Association that was published in a Prescott newspaper.

July 15, 1968
Ken W. Allen to the town of Jerome
Myself and ten other members of my family, who live in various Arizona towns, have repeatedly visited your town over the past 12 years. We always spend money there, and we always have a loaded revolver in our car because, due to the vast and often lonely and uninhabited areas that one passes through while traveling in Arizona, we feel it desirable (common sense) to have some adequate form of self-protection at hand.

Most of us ARE licensed hunters, however, in spite of that and in spite of the fact that yours is a friendly and very interesting town, we are going to avoid you like the plague so long as you have your recently passed gun ordinance. Moreover, anyone whom I can influence will do the same.

I believe your ordinance is unnecessary and based on emotionalism. I don't recall your ever having any great problem of murders or armed robberies there, so I can only mark your ordinance off as a "me too" conditioned response to the national hysteria currently in "style" on this subject [hippies].

I hope that you will see fit to rescind your gun ordinance, but if you don't you may be sure that your little ordinance has contributed toward turning America into a mediocre place of socialistic existence, rather than the place of proud self-determination that most of us have led to expect of it.

July 16, 1968. Response to Mr. Allen from the Jerome Town Council

Your letter of yesterday received this morning and I hope I can set your mind at rest regarding the recent Ordinance passed by the Council of this town ... It was not our intention when the Ordinance was passed to lend our support against any honest person using or having guns. But, no doubt you have heard of our "Hippie" situation over here. They were armed with knives, in pants and boots, chains, guns, etc., and the town was much disturbed about this as there are so many old folks around and especially women. It was felt something had to be done to protect the citizens ...

We have never stopped anyone coming into town, other than hippies ...

The Big Bee Sting

Jerome residents planted bamboo, fruit trees, and flowers. Some gardeners would pollinate their trees and flowers by hand with tiny brushes because there were no bees. Shorty Powell, who moved to Jerome in the late 1950s, planted the first black bamboo in town.

Shorty was very happy when newcomer Jerome Tweedy brought in fifteen beehives. Tweedy was a tall, blonde, skinny born-again Sikh who always wore immaculate white clothes. He set up an ashram in the Garcia House, which is now the Ghost City Inn; planted trees and a garden; and set up eight beehives in his backyard. Shorty helped find homes for the rest of the hives.

One day, Laura Williams, secretary and treasurer of the historical society, walked by and was stung when she swung her purse at the bees that buzzed near her head. Hippies made Laura quiver with rage. She referred to them as "The dirtiness."[49]

Laura marched up to Town Hall and demanded that the Jerome Town Council pass an ordinance against bees. She had a firm ally in one councilwoman, whose views of the hippies were even nastier than Laura's. The meeting was packed and old-timers and hippie newcomers squared off. The Town Council passed an ordinance that banned residents from "harboring bees or wasps."

"If they could have passed a similar ordinance against hippies, they would have done so," said Mimi Currier.

Oil and Water

It was a recipe for disaster—a needy Jerome divided against itself. The antagonism caused great turmoil. Disagreements would flare into debates that caused ill feelings, upheavals, and stalemates. The old-timers feared change and a loss of power. The town seethed with hostility. Added to the mix were volatile and sometimes petty power plays within the Town Council, fire department, and historical society.

Ordinances that banned beehives, condemned buildings, and illegal search ordinances trumped more serious problems. The water and sewer systems were on the verge of collapse. Repairs on homes and commercial businesses were an ongoing mammoth task.

Man Against the Mountain

As chaos and disorder increased, many newcomers recognized that any viable future needed cooperation, not dissension. Like the old-timers that had survived the closing of the mines, some newcomers recognized how cruel, intransigent, and unforgiving the steep mountain that they lived on could be. They volunteered on the fire department and various town boards; as money became available, they were hired to help repair walls and water and sewer lines.

"Living in Jerome is man against the mountain," said Richard Martin. He proved to be an eloquent, effective, and forceful agent of change. "You can't live here without participating or the mountain is going to push the town off the side of the hill. I think that is the thing that made us different than a lot of other hippie communities. We couldn't just sit around and party all the time. We had to pitch in to make sure water ran into our homes and toilets and sewage didn't just run down the hill. I said to myself, do we really want everything to collapse, or do we want to roll up our shirtsleeves and get involved? This led to my volunteering for Town Council. I served three times and was elected mayor twice. I did it because it needed to be done. I did it because I believed in community, which to me means finding common unity. In 1975, we were at a crossroads of thinking. Many people were responding to rational, pragmatic ideas with emotional responses that didn't mix, like oil and water. We had to learn to work together toward common goals."

Verde Exploration Buys Mingus Union High School

Paul Handverger was a board member of Verde Exploration Ltd. Although he and his wife, Berta, lived in Clarkdale, they had many friends in Jerome. Handverger still has bookcases built by Richard Martin and art from several Jerome artists on his walls.

He had seen abandoned mining towns picked over and had a great desire to see the community of Jerome succeed.

After Mingus Union High School closed in 1972, Verde Ex bought it for $25,000 and rented studios to artists. "According to a memo I wrote in that period to the board members of Verde Ex, some of the potential renters to be targeted were: artists, light industrial companies, sports facilities for the community (we did initially provide for free basketball in the gym), government training facilities (almost had a state police academy in there), and an apartment for a custodian-guard and office space," Handverger said.

In 1975, Verde Ex bought Mingus Union High School for $25,000 and targeted hippies and artists for rentals. Today it is an art studio center. Photo by Bob Swanson, www. SwansonImages.com.

"Within ten years, most of these ideas came to fruition. We let the renters put work into their spots and paid for some of their efforts with low rents and sometimes donations of materials. On some occasions, we traded rent for art."

The first renter was fine arts painter Jim Rome, who had a gallery uptown and a large following. Clothing designer Ava Guitterez was second; she eventually opened a shop on Main Street. Artists Margo Mandette and Robin Anderson rented Building C and turned it into a showpiece gallery and studio. Don Bassett, an artist who made humorous assemblages from iron scrap and bed springs, was given a small apartment and free rent in exchange for being caretaker. They were among the first artists to show that art could draw tourists to Jerome and make a profit.

Verde Ex Targets Hippies as Potential Property Owners

Handverger tried to persuade Verde Ex's board and William Golden, chairman of the board, to sell the homes and lots that Verde Ex still owned in 1977. He felt that his obligation as a Verde Ex board member was to help make their Jerome properties at least pay for themselves.

"We could get at least 250 million dollars," said Handverger, a sum Golden scoffed at. "Those properties will get fixed up and enhance the rest of what we own," Handverger argued. Finally, Golden agreed.

Many newcomers bought inexpensive homes from Verde Ex during the 1970s, but they had to pay land use fees because they could not buy the land. That policy did not provide much incentive to renovate the houses.

Handverger made a deal with the State of Arizona. The state granted permission for Verde Ex to make a one-time sale of its properties and thereby not subvert state and local subdivision regulations. He asked purchasers to buy as much property adjacent to their homes as they could afford because no more sales would be forthcoming. It was a one-time, now-or-never deal. The properties were valued at a price per square foot, regardless of condition. Verde Ex sold property to twenty-eight individuals in 1979. Many of them were hippies.

"We targeted hippies on purpose," Handverger said. "Being a property owner meant that owners would commit their talents, educate their kids there, update their houses, build businesses, and participate in the community as a whole. It would change their lives for the better, and it did. It would give them a permanent stake in the town. I believe the sale of property contributed to a major turning point in making Jerome a vibrant and successful town."

Artists Pam Fullerton and Gary Romig moved into a sweet two-room house on the steep Gulch hillside in the 1970s and bought the land from Verde Ex. "I used to love to sit on the porch, eat breakfast, and listen to Ed Dowling and Lee Downey play bluegrass music in the house below us on Gulch Road. When musician Kathleen Williamson bought the house, we'd listen to her play as well. I remember Gandalf the peacock adding his voice to the concerts." Quote and illustration by Pam Fullerton.

The "Hippie Critters" of Jerome

How the community defined itself or envisioned itself was always as quirky and fun as its residents.

Twinkle Town
Rebels without a Clue
400 people and 1000 opinions
An unintentional community
The last of the Bohemian ghettos
Large hippie coffeehouse
Only place I know of where you can spit a block
The avant-garde of the backwash
Retirement community for hippies
Floating galaxy on the mountain
A hippie redoubt
The town that died and went to heaven
A den of pirates
Where eccentricity seems commonplace
Boarding house for the voluntarily insane
Town full of hippiecritters and cocationers
Rest home for old retreads
Insane asylum without a roof

Seven
The Company Hill Houses

The most hazardous firetraps in Jerome in the 1970s were the decrepit Victorian-looking wooden houses across the street from the Catholic church. William Andrews Clark, owner of the United Verde Mine, had the homes built in the early 1900s for company managers and their families and their personal staff of housekeepers, nannies, and chauffeurs. The area was called the Upper Verde Public Utilities Plant and Housing. The old-timers called them management housing.

During a particularly severe storm in the early 1950s, one of the large drainage pipes above company hill filled with debris. When it blew out, a large amount of water torpedoed into some of the company hill houses and destroyed them. Water launched the white 1950 Dodge sedan belonging to Father John into the side of one of the larger homes. Courtesy Jerome Historical Society (90-245-2).

Just below the houses were the United Verde Apartments, which were covered by ivy that gave the illusion the apartments were in better condition than they actually were. Jerome kids liked to break in and ride the dumbwaiters.

The houses and apartments had been empty since Phelps Dodge closed the mine in 1953. One of the last to leave was teacher Jimmie Thomas and a member of the Jerome Historical Society who told me: "Heck I didn't want to leave. I had the best spot in Jerome. The entrance was on the boardwalk, a narrow walkway. My house was on stilts and went back into the hill. We had a beautiful view of the valley. The whole hill was the playground for my sister and me. We were mountain goats and we'd go up there and build a little fire and make weenies and potatoes. I've been here since I was four years old, when Main Street was still dirt. I used to lose my rubbers when it would get gooey."

Some houses settled into the soft earth and tilted until they fell over. Many had collapsed roofs. The retaining walls that were the backbone of the drainage systems on Cleopatra Mountain collapsed and allowed mudslides to slam into several homes. The wooden boardwalk in front of the lowest row of houses was badly decayed and unsafe to walk on.

The rundown houses became symbols of the ghost city. Artists loved to paint and photograph them.

An artist, whose charcoal and paint work to capture the presence of Jerome. Photo by Art Clark from Ballad of Laughing Mountain. *Courtesy Jerome Historical Society (2003-076-046).*

The homes were difficult to protect because they were isolated from more occupied sections of the town. Although doors and windows were covered with corrugated tin, and signs warned people of rattlesnakes, vandals tore off doors and broke windows to get in. Every month, a lintel here, a cornice there, some old iron work, a claw-foot bathtub, a piece of redwood siding vanished.

Only fifteen out of a total of fifty-five homes that were considered livable remained by 1972 (one a duplex). The Jerome Historical Society asked Phelps Dodge for a lease of the houses and the United Verde Apartments so they could be preserved. The society argued that if nothing was done to protect them, they would rot into the ground and leave an ugly, hazardous hole, as well as a historical gap.

Phelps Dodge stonewalled. The society decided to make one last effort to pursue that goal in 1973 and voted to send a three-member committee to Douglas, Arizona, to meet with Phelps Dodge's general manager. The company relented before the meeting could take place.

The society and Phelps Dodge signed a ten-year lease, with an option to renew, for the fifteen homes and the United Verde Apartments. The lease made reference to their "deteriorated and hazardous condition, both inside and out."[50]

The lease agreement required that the society "safeguard the United Verde Apartments and all of the residences leased herein from further damage and to make adequate provisions to prevent entry into any of the structures by any member of the public until the structure has been made safe as determined by the town of Jerome Building Inspector." Phelps Dodge required the society to take out fire and liability insurance and maintain flood control ditches.

The Company Hill houses that were not lived in collapsed. Richard Martin harvested the chimney from this one and used it for a walkway. Photo by Bob Swanson, www. SwansonImages.com

Unfortunately, the society gave little thought about how to effectively manage and fund the new responsibilities that the lease conveyed. Their budget for restoration was less than $7,500 and most of that was spent on the buildings they owned.

Lofty and Controversial Dreams for Restoration

Richard Moll, Jerome's town clerk, had lofty visions for the restoration of the deteriorated buildings. He formed The Jerome Centennial & Restoration Commission (RESTOCOM), a nonprofit corporation that issued and managed leases on behalf of the Jerome Historical Society.[51]

Moll was president. Other members were Paul Gross, mayor of Jerome and owner of the Candy Kitchen restaurant, Ruth Kruse, vice president of the Jerome Historical Society, and Helen Troyer, a past board member of the Jerome Historical Society. This was a conservative, trusted group in the society's eyes.

RESTOCOM's goal was to authentically restore the homes and the United Verde Apartments in time for America's bicentennial celebration in 1976 and to provide tours to visitors. The Tally House, once the grand home of Robert E. Tally, the United Verde mine's powerful general manager, and other homes would "be restored to house visiting dignitaries from all over the world. Formal dinners, parties, and receptions will be given in some of the mansions from time to time with honored guests arriving in an elegant antique horse-drawn surrey."[52]

Their hope was to fund these projects by raising half-a-million dollars in private and government funding. Moll dubbed the neighborhood Society Hill, and later as Company Hill.

RESTOCOM drew up an ambitious lease agreement to be signed by each caretaker. Before any caretaker moved in, the house was to have a stable foundation, basic plumbing and up-to-code electrical wiring, outside doors, safe chimney, and repair of boardwalks, all within seven months of signing the lease. In the second year, the roof was to be brought "to a finished, water-tight condition" and in the third year, exterior woodwork should be "brought to its original condition." During the fourth year, the exteriors were to be scraped and painted.[53]

The caretaker would pay fifty dollars a month or the equivalent in labor and provide monthly reports of the improvements made to RESTOCOM, which in turn would provide reports to the Jerome Historical Society. The lease stated that fixtures, such as sinks, toilets, electrical fixtures, etc., belonged to RESTOCOM, but appliances, furniture, and personal items belonged to the caretaker. Each caretaker would be responsible for fire and liability insurance in the building they occupied.

RESTOCOM would screen applicants and ask the Jerome Historical Society to approve them.

The lease provisions were just what the Jerome Historical Society wanted to hear. It gave them some assurance that the properties would be responsibly and reliably managed and provided a vision no one could argue with.

The gulf between hope and practice became obvious in the first few months and it widened to chaos in the oncoming years.

The Tally House

The funds derived from grants, donations, and potlucks were nowhere near enough to fulfill RESTOCOM's ambitious goals. During the first four years, only four applicants applied for caretaker positions. The only home to receive any grant money was the Tally House. The $7,500 it received was enough to hire three hippies to start substantial repairs to the downstairs living room and dining room and some repairs to upper floor rooms. The work included rewiring, repairs to sewer and water lines, and new plumbing fixtures. The wood floors on the first floor were repaired and refinished, woodwork and trim was restored. The beautiful wood staircases and balustrade that lead to the ballroom on the second floor was restored. The living and dining rooms were repaired, plastered, and painted, as were the bookcases and window seats. Ninety-nine panes of glass were installed.

The Tally House project was complete enough by 1976 to invite Arizona's governor and other dignitaries to a party to celebrate the American Bicentennial and Jerome's designation as a National Historic Landmark. It was the first party where members of the hippie community got to drink champagne with old-timers and visiting dignitaries. The high level of craftsmanship evident in the restoration received a great deal of praise. It gave the society and the town some confidence that the other homes would be similarly repaired.

The Tally House was formally leased for occupancy in October 1978.

The Caretakers of Society Hill

The other houses were in dire straits and needed tens of thousands of dollars of labor and materials to even begin to make them livable.

One of the many distinguished residents of this three-story house, Robert E. Tally, worked himself up in the mining company. Tally rose from mining engineer to general manager, and became president of United Verde Copper Company in 1929. Drawings by Bassett, www. jeromeartistannebassett.com.

Few caretakers applied. Caretakers were vulnerable to being thrown out at any time for not fulfilling the terms of RESTOCOM'S untenable lease requirements. The caretakers had no guarantees that they could continue to live in the houses. Nor were there any guarantees Phelps Dodge would renew the leases with the historical society.

Restoration could not be realistically accomplished under the terms of RESTOCOM's lease or its exceptionally lenient rent terms of fifty dollars a month or work-in-trade because someone could easily use up a few month's rent in glazing and reinstalling windows or unclogging and repairing sewer lines and water pipes.

RESTOCOM did what was practical. It offered to lease the homes to anyone that would be willing to live in them for sweat equity, so long as they made monthly reports about what they did.

Four hippies applied to be caretakers from 1974 to 1977. Six more caretakers were accepted in 1978, four of them hippies. A policeman leased the

Tally House and a piano tuner leased the Telegraph House. Three houses did not have caretakers until 1980, and one house never had an applicant.

Richard Moll moved away in 1975. The original set of RESTOCOM officers were replaced within two years. Some caretakers became officers and members of RESTOCOM. For the next ten years, RESTOCOM would have a different chairman every year, which made the communications between RESTOCOM and the Jerome Historical Society difficult and rancorous.

The society was suspicious of the accuracy of the monthly reports and felt some caretakers scammed the system. They felt they had no control over what repairs happened and when.

Most of the monthly reports for the first four years were sketchy at best and the hippies in control were not good at communicating with the society. For the first two or three years, reports told about cleaning up damage outside the houses, including throwing out debris, mud and boulders, excavation and leveling beneath foundations, boardwalk repairs, and repair of retaining walls. One month's report read "back bath repaired and two more windows reglazed"; another report told of a toilet installation and the rewiring of a bathroom or kitchen.[54]

Plumbing received more attention than electrical work: "Installed hot water to shower and sink," "unclogged sewer lines," "installed bathtub." Caretakers told about bringing heat to the homes: "cleaned and stabilized chimney" and "installed wood stove."[55]

The reports told a great deal about the perilous conditions of these homes, the poor conditions caretakers lived in, and the amount of work they put in to make them livable. It was cheap, but hard living. Repairs were made, just not as rapidly or up to the standards proposed by the RESTO-COM lease terms.

The society tried to take firmer control of the leases and demanded written applications from RESTOCOM. "If the written application is not adhered to, then the society has the right to void the lease."[56]

They tried to appoint a representative to attend RESTOCOM's meetings to "foster better communication." They demanded more accountability and proposed to make inspections about the monthly reports that caretakers wrote. As years went by and RESTOCOM officers became more responsible, reports got a little more detailed.

An unspoken truce settled between the society and RESTOCOM. As years passed, it became obvious that the caretakers had protected the houses from further deterioration, stabilized them, and stopped the vandalism—

My House, Magnolia Street, Jerome

Bassett ©1990

Artist Anne Bassett's company hill house. "For about ten years I lived in two rooms while doing foundation work. One is the add-on at the right, and the other a kitchen with a shed roof over it. I shoveled snow from what was to become a studio and living room. My view is awesome!" Drawings by Bassett, www.jeromeartistannebassett.com.

exactly what inspired the historical society to acquire the leases from Phelps Dodge in the first place and try to save them.

Phelps Dodge renewed the society's leases for the houses and United Verde Apartments in 1983.

Caretakers Purchase the Company Hill Houses

In 1988, the caretaker for the Tally House, who also worked for Phelps Dodge, found out that it was planning to sell all of the Company Hill houses and the United Verde Apartments for $320,000. Phelps Dodge (PD) had made a prospectus with the headline "Discover a Treasure More Valuable Than Gold" that lauded the great condition of the houses and showed exterior photos of two.

The caretaker got boiling mad at the misrepresentations made by the prospectus and the fact that PD did not have the courtesy to tell any members of RESTOCOM or the Jerome Historical Society that the property was up for sale.

RESTOCOM members took photographs of exteriors and interiors that were still in poor condition and made up their own prospectus. The caretakers knit themselves into an amicable, cohesive force, hired a lawyer, and made a counter offer to Phelps Dodge for $220,000. Within days, Phelps Dodge countered with $270,000. The terms of the sale were a small down payment; two mortgage payments a year; and a large balloon at the end of seven years. The deal included some empty lots but excluded the United Verde Apartments, which was sold separately. The caretakers' diligence and hard work had paid off and they would get to stay in their houses. They were free from the yoke of the historical society. They were thrilled.

RESTOCOM changed its name to the Society Hill Preservation Organization (SHPO—not to be confused with Arizona's State Historic Preservation Office). They drew up an agreement that held ownership of the entire property in common. They calculated the value of each house according to square footage and how long the caretaker had lived in it in order to determine mortgage payments. The empty lots were valued separately and if they were sold, the money would be split among owners in the same proportions as those used to calculate mortgage payments. The agreement allowed caretakers to sell their homes according to the payments they made and the value of the house. SHPO decided to collect three payments per year, two for Phelps Dodge, and one to be placed into savings to make the balloon payment at the end of seven years.

One of the caretakers, Ellen Smith, said "I think Phelps Dodge thought they were dealing with a bunch of hippies on the hill and that they would have the houses back when we couldn't make the balloon payment at the end. We knew we would have to depend on everyone to make payments and work together for the good of all of us. Most of the time it worked very well."

The agreement gave each house one vote, no matter how large or small the house was. The electric, water, gas, and garbage bills would be split according to the square-footage shares.

The Love Fest on Company Hill Dissolves

Disputes that centered around the boardwalk on Paradise Lane began almost as soon as the SHPO agreements were signed. The narrow wooden boardwalk provided the only front door access to houses on the lane. There was no road. Owners either parked in the parking lot behind the United Verde Apartments and walked up to the boardwalk on a steep staircase, or they accessed the boardwalk from County Lane, the steep cobblestone street that led past the Holy Family Catholic Church, or they constructed a set of steps down to their houses from Magnolia Avenue and installed a back door for their main entrance. All of the choices meant parking their cars a fair distance from their houses.

According to the SHPO agreement, owners of homes on the board-walk had responsibility for repairing the portion in front of their houses. As soon as SHPO took ownership, the owners of the house that had access from County Lane took up their portion of the boardwalk and claimed it had never existed, blocking off access to homes on the boardwalk.

There was neither will nor money to sue them, but it eroded the good-will that existed among the caretakers.

A year or so later, the United Verde Apartments were sold. The new apartment owners put up a locked chain link fence around their parking lot and a "No Trespassing" sign. No parking and no more walking up the steps to Paradise Lane.

The elegance of company hill and the United Verde Apartments (three square buildings, center) in Jerome's mining heydays. The T.F. Miller building and the O'Keefe building (lower right) were demolished by Phelps Dodge in 1953. Because the women that lived in the homes didn't venture into town due to all the saloons and rowdy single men, someone would come up and take their grocery and clothing orders and deliver them later in the day. Courtesy Jerome Historical Society (UVHVY-08-1).

It seemed to be part of a new mindset, "What's mine is mine."

Two residents on Paradise Lane took bolt cutters to the chain and the fight was on, to sue or not to sue. After some drag-out fights within SHPO, members voted to sue. And part of the new divisiveness that was engendered during that fight involved the one house, one vote agreement. The owners with the smallest homes, most of them on Paradise Lane, would bear a lesser monetary burden of the suit. Even though they were in the minority of those that desired it, the owners of the larger homes would bear greater financial responsibility. The lawsuit cost SHPO many thousands of dollars. Two years later, the judge refused to rule and told the parties to work it out. The owners of the apartments voluntarily granted access.

That lawsuit set the stage for some SHPO members to move to dissolve the organization entirely so they could acquire separate titles to their homes. Members also continued to wrangle over such issues as to how to pay for new gas lines and the repair of a collapsed wall.

The wrangling came to a head when one of the members wanted to sell the home she purchased for less than $30,000, for $200,000. Jerome's real estate boom was on by then. Some houses and Main Street businesses sold for half a million dollars.

One day, a couple from Scottsdale put in an offer for the home, but wanted clear title, which could not be given without dissolving SHPO. The couple decided to up the ante. They offered to buy a few empty lots and a nearly collapsed house that SHPO held in common for an additional $150,000, but again, only if they were given clear title. The money from the sale of the lots would be split among all SHPO members. It was enough money to sway a majority to vote for dissolution.

Eight
Rescuing the Fire Department

Fear of fire was constant as the town's residences and commercial buildings deteriorated. The abandoned houses were fire hazards and invitations to vandalism and pilfering. The fifteen Victorian homes on the hill across from the Catholic Church were particularly vulnerable because they were unoccupied.

There was a rash of fires in the early 1970s—the grocery store in Deception Gulch caught fire; a house on School Street burned to the foundation; and another on 4th or 5th Street was destroyed. Rumors were that there was an arsonist on the loose. Two houses burned in Deception Gulch. Those fires were attributed to a hippie woman's carelessness with candles. Another fire flared in the candle maker's shop on Main Street.

"The rash of fires was the turnaround that made younger people like me feel we had to get in there and participate," said Dave Hall. "I said to myself, If I'm going to live in a town this hazardous, I should be willing to join the fire department and help put out fires. And I have to tell you this: I was afraid of fire. Fire scared the hell out of me."[57]

When Hall and some of his peers first attended the fire department meetings the old-timers met them with hostility. Tensions ran high.

"They weren't too happy with the hippies joining up or criticizing them for not being progressive or safety-oriented enough," said Hall. They'd say, 'We fought fires in t-shirts. What's wrong with that?'

"Frank Farrell, a member of the fire department, would sit at Paul and Jerry's Saloon and rant, "If my house caught on fire, I wouldn't let one of those damn hippies near it. I would let it burn."

There was a real culture clash, but no physical violence. "In all fairness, those old-timers knew how to get in there and use what they had," Hall said. "They kept the town from burning down in the lean years. I was told of a fire near my house several years before I moved there. The house got struck by lightning in an August monsoon storm. Robert Sandoval, one of the old-timers who was chief then, got there, took one of the hoses out of a nearby hose box, hooked one end to the hydrant and the other to a smooth bore nozzle, and put out that fire by himself."

The Jerome Volunteer Fire Department in 1954. Most of the men are over fifty years old. Front row left to right: Postmaster Richard Lawrence, Jim Cambruzzi, Kenneth Conway (seated), Bob Lapp, Charlie Williams (seated), Earl Connor, Jerry Sullivan, Mayor John McMillan, and Dominic Beneitone. Back row left to right: Pete Yurkovich, Dr. Joe Pecharich, and Earl Bell. Courtesy Jerome State Historic Park.

Phil Tovrea was nominated for fire chief in 1975 against Tony Lozano, one of the old-timers. Tovrea was a member of one of Arizona's most illustrious cattle baron families, but he was a renegade who ran away to Jerome. Robert Sandoval, the former fire chief, moved to Cottonwood. Phil remembers that when he won the election, the old-timers seemed somewhat relieved. Phil instituted a policy that demanded the department train every week and dismissed people who did not show up. There were no old-timers on the fire department after 1976.

Peggy Tovrea, Debbie Hall, and Jane Moore started the fireman's auxiliary after the election. They sponsored Halloween dances to raise funds for needed equipment and silk-screened t-shirts at Phil and Peggy's house.

Fighting Fires with No Water and Poor Equipment

When Tovrea became fire chief, the town's water system was near collapse. There was concern about how to maintain a regular flow of water into Jerome and how to make sure there was enough of it to put out fires. John

McMillan knew how fast fires would "drain those tanks when they were plumb full of water."[58]

There were times when water was not coming into Jerome at all. "We had to have tanker trucks bring water up here because the lines were so holey the water was not getting to town," said Jane Moore, a member of the firemen's auxiliary.[59]

The second concern was how to adequately equip the fire department. When Phil Tovrea took over, there were two 1928 and 1937 Dodge fire trucks, four sets of petrified fire coats, no radio equipment, brittle hoses from the 1920s, and an unregulated high-pressure hydrant system with rotten pipes. There was a public phone on the outside wall of Paul and Jerry's Saloon that rang when citizens reported a fire. Whoever was nearby would call a fireman to tell him to set off the fire alarm sirens on the roofs of Town Hall and the Hotel Jerome and alert the department. The phone also rang at the fire chief's home.

"It was all so inadequate and scary," said Hall. "To his credit, when Tony Lozano was fire chief, he did start some movement toward modernization. He began a fundraiser called Mining Daze, with contests and a

The Jerome Volunteer Fire Department in 1976. All hippie newcomers. Note new gear and hard hats on some. Lower left to right: Ron Ballatore, Jim Kinsella, Dave Ahern, Irene Baxter, Dave Hall, and John Tudan. Back row left to right: Dave Moore, Vince Henry, Kim Talbot, Phil Tovrea, Joanne McKeever, Kathleen Williamson, and unidentified tourist behind. Courtesy Jerome State Historic Park.

dance afterward, and that money got put aside to buy a new truck. By 1974, other community organizations threw in money and in 1975, when Tovrea was elected, the fire department had enough money to buy a brand new green Ford ¾-ton pickup truck. We installed a pump and tank in the bed."

Carmen Kotting was one of two new firefighters that volunteered in the late 1970s. "Just after I got on the department there was a fire on Diaz Street. Nobody showed up when the alarm went off, so I jumped in the '28 truck. It had a bent seat and I had to stand up on the pedals. Going down hill, I had to double-clutch and pray the brakes would hold. By the time I got to the fire, my knees were jelly. Then others came and we hosed the fire out."

The Fire That Could Have Spelled Disaster

The first big fire that was fought by the new department was in 1976. The fire was at the Hostetter's home near the Douglas Mansion. Artist Jim Rome and Jerry Vojnic were in Paul and Jerry's Saloon when the siren went off. They grabbed the new truck and sped down the hill. The other firemen grabbed the older trucks. Jane Moore and Shirley McClain watched the fire with great trepidation from the porch at the Cuban Queen. "Paul Gross, who was mayor of Jerome, kept the Candy Kitchen open all night for firefighters to take breaks and their families to hang out for news of the fire," Jane said.

Dave Hall described what happened.

"The whole place was in flames when we got there. Minnie Hostetter was leaning out the second story window and had to jump because no one could get the ladder up to her in time and she broke an ankle. The truck's pump had lost its prime and no one knew how to re-prime it.

"Doc Moore and I grabbed a line from the small truck and Tovrea hooked it up to the hydrant only to find there was no water. The fire just kept right on burning. Doc Moore and Craig McLain almost got into the house when one of the door lintels fell in. We did manage to get several dogs out of the basement before we started hearing the pop, pop, pop of what sounded like bullets going off from the fire's heat and we just ran and hid in a gulley. Finally, the Cottonwood and Clarkdale fire trucks showed up. We extended some hose lines down to a hydrant by the Douglas Mansion and finally got some water. The fire burned through the night and finally went out early in the morning.

"That fire was a real comedy of errors, but it served as a huge wake-up call. That fire showed everyone how much we had to learn and how much our old equipment had to be repaired or replaced. Luckily, the only fireman who got hurt was Guy Henley who burned his hand. Phil Tovrea was the driving force for rescuing the fire department and getting us trained up and lobbying for better equipment. He did the community a real service."

A New Fire Station

In two decades, Jerome had an adequately equipped and manned fire department and enough funds to pay a part-time chief. The town of Jerome had begun to be savvy about getting grants and fund-raising. In 1996, the Jerome Town Council voted to build a new fire station. Lee Christensen, a long-time resident, was the architect. The handsome two-story building was finished in 1998 at a cost of approximately $350,000. By then, Jerome was well into becoming a tourist boomtown.

Drawing of the new fire station. Drawings by Bassett, www.jeromeartistannebassett.com.

Nine
Rebuilding the Water and Sewer Systems

Jerome had sophisticated water, sewer, and drainage systems and extensive retaining walls that served the mines, houses, schools, hospital, and businesses of the city of 15,000 residents. These systems were engineering and architectural feats, models for their era. Regularly scheduled maintenance of those systems, and the funds to provide it, came to an abrupt halt when the mines closed.[60]

Volunteers dealt with the problems that surfaced for the next two decades. If a water line leaked somewhere on the mountain, someone would trudge up to patch it with tire tubes. When new water pipe was needed, the Jerome Historical Society would donate funds and Phelps Dodge would donate surplus eight-inch steel pipe.

Cast-iron pipe was scrounged to make repairs when sewage spilled down the hillside.

Collapse of the water and sewer systems seemed imminent in 1975. The town of Jerome was nearly broke. It was one of the poorest towns in Arizona.

The preservation of historical buildings was a dominant theme of Jerome's first act as a village. Rescue of its infrastructure was dominant in the second. Without a total overhaul, Jerome was headed for complete decay into the ghost city it claimed to be.

The newcomers pitched in to help, and with the exuberance of youth, built the bridge that connected them to older residents. They volunteered for positions on the fire department, the historical society, and town government. The necessity of finding and repairing the water and sewer systems brought newcomers and old-timers together. "Many of us still remember the day the water quit working in Jerome and our toilets would no longer flush," said Richard Martin.

"We may have lacked knowledge and experience, but not smarts," said Doyle Vines, who worked various jobs for the town of Jerome for eight years. "All of us learned on the job. That was the beauty of freedom. When people have freedom and there is great need, they find ways to get done what needs to be done. We moved into our broken-down homes into a broken-down town and began to participate. We found it within ourselves to take responsibility on our own backs, getting bruised, both physically and emotionally in the process, and chose to just keep on going. All recognized one overriding commonality: a passionate love for the town that transcended personal gain. The vitality of the town was the driving force in the new community life we built."[61]

"The way I felt about it, I kind of resented it at first, this hippie group moving in," said John McMillan when a Canadian reporter interviewed him in 1984. "[They were] a bunch of knuckleheads who were too damn lazy to shave and never took a bath and that sort of stuff. But I found there were some pretty smart kids among them and they got into the politics of Jerome and took over the Town Council and did a pretty good job. I don't resent that at all because these old-timers, they can't run the damn place forever."[62]

Rescuing the Water System

Water flowed to Jerome from seventeen permanent and intermittent springs on Mingus Mountain. The main pipeline was a 70,000-foot anaconda that coiled down the mountain and traversed four wooden trestles that spanned the steep canyons. The water flowed into storage tanks that were located above the mining operations and from there into Jerome.

Water that was not used overflowed into a large drainage ditch through town into Bitter Creek. Jerome residents always knew when flow was low because there would be no water in the ditch.

The water from the springs was quite pure, uncontaminated by the pollutants that plagued other mining towns, and was seemingly inexhaustible. Although Phelps Dodge had a stake in keeping the water system operating after they closed their mine, they formally washed their hands of maintaining the lines sometime in the 1960s, when they handed responsibility to the town of Jerome.

One of four wooden trestle bridges that held the main water pipeline coiling down to Jerome from a spring located twelve miles away. Courtesy Jerome Historical Society (P-1990-135-044).

When Jerome volunteers first walked the lines with their tools, they did not know what to expect. "They'd find two or three different types of pipe, not all of them equal in diameter, and all of them would be leaking," said Doyle Vines. "As deeply buried as the pipeline once was, erosion caused large sections of it to be exposed above ground. The exposed joints would rust and break, water would pool near breakages, rabbits and mice would get into the pipes, contaminating the water and making it necessary for people in Jerome to boil it until the problem cleared. Desert plants would find their way into any cracks. Seven- to eight-inch long root balls would be brought in to council meetings to demonstrate how unruly these plants were. The joints were also susceptible to breakage because of large 'burps' in pressure caused by intermittent springs kicking in after snowmelt or big rains. Pieces of broken wooden trestles constantly needed shoring up."

The pressure changes would occasionally cause water heaters to burst in homes and commercial buildings.

The aggressive roots of the Paradise trees explored cracks in the water and sewer lines. They toppled retaining walls and undermined foundations. These trees grew with such ferocity and abundance that a botanist who presented a symposium on *Ailanthus* in 1989 for the Jerome Historical Society described Jerome as a town within a forest that needed to be managed.[63]

The water that used to flow pure and clean became muddy and prone to contamination and eventually the town had to chlorinate it.

The Ghost of Duke Cannell

This remembrance of Duke Cannell is excerpted with permission from an unpublished story written by Richard Martin, his "hippie friend."

"After I had lived in Jerome for a while, I came to realize that in order to get along with the 'locals,' as well as eat, you had to work. Not only did you have to work, you had to make sure the locals saw you work. If you were seen working, no matter what you looked like, in my case a big guy with a head full of hair, they'd keep an eye on you. If folks liked what they saw, eventually they might venture by to say hello, get acquainted, maybe even become a little friendly.

"That's how I came to know Duke Cannell. Duke was the caretaker of the Phelps Dodge properties in Jerome and Clarkdale, operating the pumps at the big arsenic-laced tailing pond in Clarkdale, keeping an eye on the Jerome water system and running trespassers off dangerous mining properties.

"Making his daily rounds, Duke usually passed by my shop every day and would try to catch a glimpse of 'the working hippie,' as he had labeled me. Being a curious man, he finally just had to stop in to see 'what's goin' on.' Our earliest conversations were initiated with Duke saying something like, 'Say, you wouldn't mind giving me a hand to go up and work on the water line now would ya?'

"'Me?' Looking around to see if there was someone else he could be talking to. 'Sure, I'll go!'

"We'd climb into the mining company's white pickup and head off up the mountain to see if we could figure out why there was no water coming into town. I was Duke's first hippie friend and he was my first cowboy friend. I would help him repair the water lines with strips of rubber torn from old tire tubes and he'd tell me stories about the mining days.

Duke Cannell. According to Richard Martin, "Duke taught me his tricks—how to wrap a broken water line with salvaged inner tubes and sticks, prop up collapsed trestles and pipes with fallen timbers, and spot telltale green stains that indicated leaks." Courtesy Richard Martin collection.

"We'd come back to the big sandstone walls of my shop building that gathered both heat and wasps seeking warmth in the late autumn sun. Duke used to call those deep maroon walls a 'Mexican heater—you know those Mexicans, they'll lean against a wall like that all day, tryin' to stay warm.' So did I. So did Duke. Him, me, and the wasps almost every day, one foot on the wall, one on the boardwalk, talking and warming.

"Even though Duke had worked well past retirement age, he could do the work of much younger men. So he couldn't understand why Phelps Dodge told him they needed a younger caretaker. 'Why?' said Duke. 'I never could figure that out, it's not like anything was going on.' He liked his job caretaking the remains of a once mighty industrial enterprise. Duke was a caretaker.

"Sometime in the late 1980s my friend stopped coming by my shop so often, and when he did, he seemed a little smaller each time. Always cheerful, still perfectly pressed and always proud, but just a little smaller.

"Finally the visits stopped and it became my turn to visit—to stop by and make sure everything was okay. With his wife Dorothy at his side, everything was always okay. 'She's still strong enough to take her outside and prop her up to cut the firewood,' Duke loved to tell me. Except Duke was not okay. He was fading.

"One Saturday morning I decided to pay a visit to my friend on Sunshine Hill. I'd put a really nice stereo in my pickup. I pulled up to the little house and parked behind Duke's shiny pickup, now covered with a layer of dust. I opened both doors of my truck and popped in a stereo tape of narrow gauge steam trains climbing the Colorado Mountain passes. I turned it up as loud as I thought I could get away with.

"The trains chugged and chuffed, clattered and whistled.

"The screen door swung open, and a little, bent man in his bathrobe stepped out on the porch with a big smile and those twinkling eyes. No Stetson that morning, just thin white hair combed just right. Just like a gentleman.

"We sat on the oak swing that Chuck, my partner in the cabinet shop, and I had built for Duke and Dorothy, together we sat back and forth gently swinging, and listening to the trains passing by.

"A few weeks later I was filling my truck with gasoline at the mini-mart at the bottom of the hill from Jerome. My neighbor, Jane, pulled in and stopped, stepping out of her car, with a serious face she looked at me and said. 'Did you hear about Duke?'

"'No.' My heart skipped, she need say no more.

"'He shot himself yesterday. Fireman Jim Kinsella found him.'

"Several days after Duke's funeral, I stopped by the house to see how things were going for Dorothy.

"'Duke told me that it was getting too hard to live up here in Jerome, what with the mountains, and the stairs, and his failing health. He told me that I should find a place in the valley for me to live. When he said that, I wondered what he meant by that, where 'I' should live. The day that he died he told me to go look at a place in the valley that we found in a newspaper ad. I decided to do that. He was probably right. So I left to go look for the place. Just before I got to the stop sign in town, I felt like my heart just exploded. When I got back home, I couldn't find Duke ... and I didn't want to look. I knew he was gone. I called the fire department.'

"She cried. So did I."[64]

Financing Water Repairs

Rubber inner tubes were only temporary bandages. Leaks multiplied exponentially and a great deal of water was lost. Jerome's water pipes had so many leaks in the mid-1970s that although the springs produced a flow of 650 gallons per minute (gpm), the flow into town was only 60 gpm, if that—a flow so low that restaurants and bars often closed.

The only valid solution was to replace the pipe. However, lack of funds made that solution difficult, particularly for a town that constantly ran in the red. Almost every day revealed a new crisis to fund.

A plan to raise some 1.2 million dollars from a combination of bonds ($400,000) and grants ($800,000) was put forward in 1975 under the leadership and vision of Mayor Paul Gross.

Michael Smith, publisher and editor of *The Jerome Magician* wrote, "If you want to continue to have water at all and would like to have water available at the fire hydrants also, get out and vote yes for the $50,000 water improvement bonds and the $350,000 water revenue bonds." Some of the debt service for one of the bonds would accrue to Jerome property tax payers, based on assessed valuations. The measure overwhelmingly passed.

It would take six successive town councils twelve years to get the water system to perform with regularity and ease. A town crew of hippie newcomers accomplished the work.

The work of repair and pipe replacement was scheduled in three phases. Phase one repaired or replaced the water line from Walnut Springs about

One of the concrete ditches for water overflowing from water tanks above Jerome. When there is no water flowing in the ditch, the Jerome town manager asks for conservation. Photo by Bob Swanson, www. SwansonImages.com

three miles from Jerome to repairs to the storage tank adjacent to the open pit. Phase two repaired or replaced the water line from Walnut Springs back to and above the siphon. The major distribution system in downtown Jerome was repaired or replaced at the same time. Phase three repaired or replaced the remaining portions of the transmission system. New pipes were installed in Deception Gulch and the area known as the hogback.

The grants and bonds supplied money in 1978 for part-time help. Richard Martin was mayor; Doyle Vines was zoning law enforcer and historic preservation manager. Ron Ballatore was town manager and chief of police. Lew Currier was hired as town clerk.

It was up to Doyle and Ron to schedule repairs and pipe replacement. They had to figure out where all the lines were and how to deal with the fluctuations in water pressure when the intermittent springs kicked in and shot the pressure up eight or ten times higher than what the pipes normally carried.

What helped the most was that Doyle discovered a paper called "The Hydrology of Jerome," written in 1912, together with maps that showed where the surges in pressure were likely to be. The information enabled

Ron to design a system of pressure regulators and custom valves to bleed off air and prevent pressure surges.

The Shoebox Full of Bills

Lew Currier was hired by the town of Jerome to deal with accounting for the money from the water bonds and grants that was spent. Each source of funds was administered by a different federal or state entity. Some funds went to revenues; others to repairs or future repairs; another to expansion; another to replacement of lines; still another went to deferment of payment of interest on the bond; and another was for subcontractors, engineering, and legal. Reports had to be filed in a timely and professional manner.

The gap between what was supposed to happen and what was actually going on was clear from Currier's first day on the job. "I was given a shoebox full of bills that had to be paid and some checkbooks," he said. "Where's the general ledger? I asked. No one seemed to know what a general ledger was. There was no system, no accounts payables, no organized method of accounting for grant funds. I was told to pay the oldest bills first and 'see what was left.' What money there was went for pipelines and maintenance and other emergencies and we were always running behind. Many of our vendors hadn't been paid in more than 120 days."

The difficulties were compounded by the lack of cooperation from people that still resented the hippies. Three residents sued the town for failure to file annual audits—they had just lost their bid for election to the Town Council. They also accused the town of misappropriation of funds.

"They disliked the hippies and were always on our backs," said Lew. "But they were also right. There hadn't been an audit in many years, way before any hippies got on the council, and maybe not since the mines closed. They were wrong about funds being misappropriated. We had documentation enough for the last few years to prove that no money had been misappropriated. There just was not that much to go around. And we were also proud of the fact that for the first time in recent history, the town was out of debt and current with all its bills.

"For a while, getting accounting systems in place was a merry-go-round," Currier said. "Until the town got a general ledger system, the town couldn't have an audit. Until the town built up their reserve accounts for the bonds and grants they had, no more grants could be applied for. It took a few years to get the accounts and reporting methods straightened out, before an actual audit could be conducted."

Once this occurred, new grants were found to replace some water storage tanks and add new ones above the town.

Doyle added, "Lew did an extraordinary job creating the ledgers from scraps and notes, while dealing with everyday business and a serious revenue deficit. He also answered the phones and talked graciously with every person who came into the office, including chronic critics like Joe Marini. What he accomplished was nothing short of a miracle."

Repairing the Sewer System

No one likes to manage shit. Flush it out of sight and out of mind is how most people like to think about it. Except in Jerome. When a sewer pipe broke, shit, tampons, and toilet paper backed into toilets, spilled onto floors, and flowed into streets, yards, and washes. Paradise trees thrived on the fertilizer. The town crew had to clean out the clogged lines and repair them.

They soon found out that the condition of the sewer system was as deplorable as the water system.

My son Michael's first day on the town crew in the early 1980s included unclogging a sewer line out on Holly Street. A small skunk had gotten trapped and died. As soon as the line was free, a huge spray of sewage flew into the air and onto Michael. "The smell was unbelievable," he told me. "It took a lot of washing machine cycles to get it out of my clothes."

Not all parts of Jerome were hooked up to the main sewer system. In Deception Gulch, some of the toilets fed into an old line that went to a sand bed septic tank located at the end of the gas station at the edge of town. "Who knows when it was last mucked out," commented Doyle Vines. Sewage often ran down the hill into the wash that ended up in Clarkdale.

Other homes in the Gulch had outhouses. "In the mid-seventies, we rented a house for $25 a month that was located across the wash that we called Dogpatch," recalled Lew Currier. "There was no hookup to the sewer so we had to find an outhouse. We found an old, never used WPA one-holer in Clarkdale that was named 'Air Police' and used our old '57 Chevy pickup to cart it up to our house."

People that were living in the dilapidated homes in Mexican town below the post office lived in what old-timers referred to as a greenbelt. The yards and hillsides flourished with weeds and it was greener than most other parts of town. "The crew didn't know some of the homes weren't hooked up to the main system," Lew Currier said. "One day Esiquia Sandoval called to report her toilet was overflowing and that's how we found out she was not even hooked up. She had been paying sewer fees since the mine closed. The town refunded her the money and then hooked her up."

In the main part of Jerome (up from the high school to the street the hospital was on), the sewer pipes had become sieves. Some were ductile iron that had rusted, some plastic, and the cleanouts seemed to be located just anywhere and most were in poor repair. "There were maybe fifty or sixty sections of pipes and cleanouts needing repair," Doyle said. "Just getting to them was problematic. The town had no comprehensive view of their layout and some went under houses or roadbeds."

The town sewer system fed into transmission pipes that led to a dysfunctional sewer plant located in the wash below the Douglas Mansion. Bitter Creek flowed into it. The main priority was to get it working properly before planning how to systematically fix the town sewer lines.

Doyle Vines wrote the first grant to temporarily fix sewer lines and clean out the sewer plant. "We chose to put the grant money in wages rather than the expensive pump stations and a new road that were recommended by an engineering company. The cost of building the road would have used up all of the grant money. After much negotiation with block grant officials, the town was allowed to call it a 'repair project' and not new construction that required new engineering."

Men and women were hired, and, according to Doyle, the women worked so hard that the men were embarrassed to stop, particularly Irene Baxter and Jane Moore. Irene was a member of the fire department and Jane helped set up the fireman's auxiliary. Artist Anne Bassett volunteered to haul cement down the last two loops of the road in her Karmann Ghia. She made drawings of the new plant, and later made sure that all the crew etched their names in the cement they poured.

"The crew used shovels and picks to build a roadbed four feet wide starting from behind the Cuban Queen up town, passing down to the Powder Box Church, under the road, and down to the sewage plant so we could bury the transmission pipe to the holding tank. Along the way we built cleanouts and a pressure relief valve," Doyle said. "A lot of the materials for the plant were taken down on the backs of mules. They mucked out tons of crap and put it into a holding tank. When the liquid rises in the tank, it flows out. So the crew built new drying beds filled with small rocks to filter the liquid before it flowed out into the hillside. We killed the bacteria in these liquids with a chlorinator that was run by a paddle wheel that we installed inside the sewer line to generate electricity, which no one had done before.

"When I took the state people on a tour of the new plant, they were amazed at the innovation and backbreaking labor that had gone into it. They approved the work."

The Case of the Azure-colored Water

Jerome's mining wealth came at a big cost to the surrounding environment. Mining is a dirty business. Contaminated wastes and tailings are visible from most every part of town.

The biggest environmental threat to Jerome's sewage treatment plant was the flow of azure-colored water that came during heavy rains from drainages on Perkinsville Road between what is now the Gold King Mine and Jerome. The large slag heap and tailings on Sunshine Hill, just above the Little Daisy Hotel, leached into Bitter Creek, which flowed directly into the sewer plant and contaminated it and the groundwater below.

That water contained copper sulfate, cadmium, selenium, and arsenic.

A characteristic of sulfide ores is that they oxidize when exposed to air and water, i.e., they turn to sulfates. The toxic cocktail of blue water resulted from the oxidation of copper sulfides in the tailings piles that were created by the United Verde Mine and its successor, Phelps Dodge Corporation. Today, the colors that appear in unworked portions of the open pit above town and many of its tailings—vivid oranges, yellows, blues, dark reds—are evidence of the oxidation process, as well as indication that some ore still exists.

Kids liked to throw nails and car parts into the azure water and watch them turn copper. Jerome citizens loved to take their dogs walking out on Sunshine Hill and out Perkins Road but had to restrain them from drinking the water.

The Mining Act of 1872 regulated little in the way of environmental degradation. Mining companies had a virtual free pass to mine gold, copper, and coal as profitably as possible. Pollution caused by mining was largely ignored until 1970 when the Environmental Protection Agency (EPA) was founded.

Amendments to the Federal Water Pollution Control Act (Clean Water Act) in 1972 established guidelines for the regulation of pollutants discharged into ground and surface water. This meant that the EPA could mandate the cleanup of degraded and hazardous mining sites. The laws were strengthened when the Comprehensive Environmental Response, Compensation, and Liability Act (CERCLA or Superfund) was passed in

1980. This gave the EPA authority over sites contaminated with hazardous substances, as well as other pollutants or contaminants.

Jerome citizens complained about the toxic water to the town of Jerome and the town contacted the EPA. The new laws gave EPA officials a mandate to investigate complaints. They came to Jerome, took photographs, and passed complaints on to officials at Phelps Dodge and hoped for voluntary compliance. It did not happen. Instead, Phelps Dodge stalled the process by claiming that there were broken water pipes under the affected lands and that the town was responsible for maintaining them, a claim that was untrue.

Finally, in 2003, the EPA issued a Complaint and Consent Decree against Phelps Dodge for discharging acid mine drainage (i.e., the blue water) in violation of the Clean Water Act. Phelps Dodge was fined civil penalties of $220,000 and told to formulate a reclamation plan to stop seepage into Bitter Creek and other groundwater resources downstream.

Phelps Dodge formulated a remediation plan and spent close to $12 million to control the seepage. Phelps Dodge was sold to Freeport-McMoRan Copper and Gold, Inc., in 2006. Freeport is the largest publicly traded copper producer in the world and one of the world's largest producers of gold.[65]

Freeport continued the remediation plan begun by Phelps Dodge and spent tens of millions of dollars in 2009 and 2010 in extensive voluntary reclamation to improve water resources. Part of that project was to build a new drainage system on their property to ensure that mining wastes did not escape into groundwater resources.

The azure water stopped flowing.

Freeport also provided a much-appreciated parking lot for tourists just outside of Jerome on the road to the Gold King Mine. They also provided the use of their buildings at the 300-level to the town of Jerome for vehicle and equipment storage and to sculptor Scott Owens for a studio.

Ten
Repairing Jerome's Retaining Walls

Fifteen hundred retaining walls can be found from the top of Jerome to the bottom of Deception Gulch. They are among the town's most impressive and enduring architectural treasures.

The walls help keep homes from slipping down the mountain. They resist the downhill creep of the mountain imposed by the forces of gravity, lack of vegetation, constant water runoff, and the occasional earthquake tremor. They anchor the town to the mountain.

Jerome's retaining walls began to collapse soon after the mines abandoned the town and people started moving out. Deforestation of the mountains was a contributing cause. The Yavapai, native Americans that lived in the area before mining began, called them "Mountains of Many Trees," but they were renamed Mingus for the man who founded the company to cut the trees, and Woodchute, to commemorate the construction of the long chute that cascaded logs down the mountain. United Verde built a system of walled drainage ditches on Cleopatra Mountain to help prevent mud-slides during heavy rains, but the walls deteriorated after the mines closed. Efforts to seed the mountain with trees were unsuccessful and the ditch walls were not rebuilt. Mudslides and retaining wall failures were common throughout the town during heavy rains.

Almost everyone in Jerome has put their hands to repairing walls. The walls tell something about the resourcefulness, stubbornness, tenacity, aesthetics, and even quirky natures of their builders. When the old-timers saw the hippie newcom-

Two-tiered retaining wall built by hippies in the lower park across the street from the ruins of the old Bartlett Hotel. Photo by Bob Swanson, www.SwansonImages.com

ers rebuilding walls, they knew they had come to stay and were prepared to help shoulder some of the responsibilities for rebuilding the town.

Jerome's Hand-stacked Walls

Many walls are hand-stacked, one stone over two, much like the ancient Inca walls of Machu Picchu, and have no mortar between them. Properly built, the rocks "weep," and act as natural drains. They have an elasticity that enables them to shift and settle. Explosions shook the town during the mining days and occasional tremors occur. In 1976, a small quake shook glasses in Paul and Jerry's Saloon. The epicenter of a 3.2 quake in 1984 was located five miles outside of Jerome. It sounded like an underground train ambling through the town's underbelly. Some rocks tumbled, but the walls held.

Most rocks for Jerome's retaining walls are quarried from within a seven-mile radius of town. The walls contain rocks from the same formations that are dominant in the Grand Canyon—1.8-billion-year-old schist, maroon Tapeats sandstone that holds millions of tiny shells, limestone of the Martin Formation and cherry-streaked Redwall sandstone, the ruby-colored Supai sandstone, and black lava basalt. They convey the geology of the ancient seas that once covered the area and the tumult of volcanoes and earthquakes.

Miners built walls to hold steep hillsides back from whatever materials were at hand: old tin, boards, steel pipe, even old bedsprings. Photos by Bob Swanson, www.SwansonImages.com

Not all of Jerome's walls are made of hand-stacked rock. Immense concrete walls are found at the base of the high school, Town Hall, and the Douglas Mansion. One of the walls on Holly Street is built of railroad trestles and giant steel sheets that were used to form mine shafts. Some walls are collages that are made with just about anything that builders found laying around—discarded telephone poles, bedsprings, engine blocks, woodstove doors, corrugated tin, laundry buckets, refrigerators, and discarded tires that were filled with stone. Jerome's builders recycled almost everything long before it was fashionable.

This wall, close to a home on Gulch Road, was constructed of laundry buckets and filled with dirt. Photo by Bob Swanson, www.SwansonImages.com

Repair of the Holly Street Wall

Wall maintenance and repair was a nightmare for a town strapped for cash and manpower until the late 1970s when Jerome began to apply for and receive government grants, and young people applied for the jobs.

The first major wall to be repaired by the town of Jerome was the thirty-five foot tall by eighty-foot long highway wall that separated the

There are three different types of retaining walls on Holly Street. The wall on the left next to the upright metal wall was constructed by a team of hippies under the leadership of artist Paul Nonnast. Photo by Bob Swanson, www. SwansonImages.com.

high end of Holly Street from the State Park road directly below it. The collapsed wall jeopardized the stability of nearby homes.

The town of Jerome hired artist Paul Nonnast as foreman and a crew that included quite a few hippies. There was a lot of competition because in 1980 there was no other work around. The town paid $3.35 an hour.

Nonnast rejected the architectural plans that called for a completely vertical rock face. Instead, he had the crew angle the rocks back away from the street. The wall was divided into two parts with a narrow terrace to divide them. Giant stone steps were inset into the wall. The steps were a suggestion by crewman Richard Flagg, whose travels in Central America showed him that steps were a common feature of many ancient retaining walls. Six portholes, welded from old steel, were set into the wall to add stability and efficient drainage.

"I became a wall-builder of necessity," Nonnast told me. "With the little money I came here with, I bought an old truck and an empty lot out at the lonesome edge of town. My stone house was built with my hands, stones, pick-axes, shovels, plumb bob, and a wheelbarrow.

"Managing that crew was not easy," Nonnast said. "Few had ever done this kind of work but were desperate for work. Many of us lived on the fringe, a hard dwelling life here in those days. We had our backs up against the wall in one way or another and we were emotionally young.

"There was a lot of discord because there were some loose cannons among us. One of my jobs was to stop fights. I remember being out at the quarry with a guy named Desperado Dave. He wore a large brimmed hat and hauled railroad ties for a living. One day, Dave swung the jackhammer around and started giving everyone orders. When I told him to f*^# off, he came running at me with the jackhammer pointed like a gun. I told him I'd kill him if he got too close. That was a revelation to me. I probably would have.

"I knew we passed a milestone when one of the drunks on my crew brought his drinking buddies down from the bar to show them what we were doing. We were all proud of that wall and it drew us closer together. It showed us our interdependency."

The Great Wall of Walter

My husband, Walter, and I bought our house at the top of Gulch Canyon in 1981 for $30,000. The road ended in our backyard. The house was so dilapidated that when my mother-in-law saw it for the first time, she blurted, "You didn't have to pay for that did you?"

About six months later, we sat in our front yard after dinner and watched storm clouds mix shadows with sunlight on the valley below. Pinpoints of sunlight illuminated the jagged edges of the carmine pinnacles and clefts in the canyons across the valley. The sunset threw up shades of tangerine, pink, and amethyst. A triple rainbow appeared. A few people blew their conches in celebration and the echoes swirled around us.

We went to sleep feeling the contentment of having found a home in a beautiful place.

The rain began shortly before we went to sleep. The wind whipped itself into ferocious rumbles and high shrieks, staccato barks and odd two- and three-part harmonies that spun weird melodies. They were sounds we came to love and fear.

We woke to lightning-thrown yellow shadows in the bedroom, followed by a deafening thunderclap and then a crash. The whole house shuddered for a moment and then settled. The only sound for many minutes was the rain beating on the roof. My heart was pounding. We got up and peered out one of the windows, but it was too dark to see anything. "Let's just go back to sleep," Walt said. "We'll find out what happened in the morning."

Walt woke up first and walked to the living room window. "Shit," I heard. Half the front yard close to the foundation of our house had become a hill that sloped steeply to a jumble of rocks fifteen feet below. Rain had saturated the clay-like dirt, the weight of the hill turned the dirt to slurry, and the rocks had nothing to support them.

We went outside, in a state of shock, unprepared for the magnitude of what we saw, much less what it might mean to deal with.

Richard Martin, who lived in the house directly below ours, drove up moments later. "Welcome to Jerome," he laughed. "The crash woke me up. When I looked out this morning and saw the blowout of your wall, the first thing I felt was relief that some of the rocks didn't tumble into my house."

"Oh," we said, not even having considered that possibility.

"Everything in this town slides downward," he said. "It's why there are so few true right angles in our houses. The walls keep the town more or less together and rebuilding collapsed walls is something everyone here does. This wall is just a little more drastic."

By this time the rest of our household had gathered outside. Our eighteen-year-old son Michael said nothing. We had to grab our four-year-old son Max before he tumbled down the hill. Walt's high school friend, George, who had moved in with us and was helping put in insulation and repair windows, announced, "I don't do digging."

"Well I don't either," Walt said, pitching a sudden tantrum. "I didn't sign on to rebuild walls. I didn't sign on to move here. I'm leaving. You all can do what you want. I can't take this anymore." His face was contorted, lips pursed out, eyes narrowed. He started sobbing.

We were dumbfounded. Richard, Michael, and George shrugged their shoulders and disappeared inside. I cried.

Max pulled me back into reality: "I want breakfast." At least there was the immediacy of this task to focus on.

Up to this point, Jerome had been a playground—we were among friendly, dope-smoking hippies in a colorful mining town that had been virtually abandoned. Now, I was beginning to understand that there were emotional underpinnings that tested and challenged all of us who lived here.

The first of thirteen retaining walls that were built by Walter Rapaport. Photo by Bob Swanson, www. SwansonImages.com.

It would take seven years and approximately one hundred tons of rock for Walt to repair what became a thirty-five foot long and twelve-foot high wall. And yes, George dug and so did everyone else in the family. Many friends helped.

The rocks from the former wall got used up in laying a large foundation. Walt and friends gathered the rest from the mountains. Each stone had to be moved seven times: rolled toward the truck; lifted into the truck; dumped off the truck; rolled down one hillside; rolled down another hillside; lugged over to the spot near where it would be carefully placed into the wall, one rock over two, as our friends taught us to do.

We carefully placed rocks behind the rock face to make a tight backfill. We referred to the wall as an upside-down wall. As the wall got taller, the rocks got bigger, more Herculean. Walt grew braver and more confident; his strength was fortified through the building of something that massive.

Walt hated the wall at the start but ended up feeling a deep kinship with it. He rebuilt ten massive walls on our 80x100-foot lot, and isolated the house in the center of massive ramparts, his stand against the mountain. From a distance they look like the old Anasazi walls he liked to spend time looking at on his many hikes.

"When you build walls, every day is an invention. There comes a point in the process where I see what the wall wants to look like at the end, and up until that point, I have no idea, the aesthetic isn't planned and I don't have a goal, I'm just building the wall for a particular purpose with the rocks at hand. At some point the wall itself builds energy and the rocks seem to choose themselves and direct me to put them where they want to be. And when you lay a rock down, even if it is in the wrong place, it will stay patient until it is moved to the next place. The rocks tell me where they want to go. At that point I am no longer the director but the directee of the wall that I am building. It has to do with the way the earth is. Some walls tell you to follow their contours; others tell you to go against them, but either way, there is always the need to follow the lay of the earth. Rocks are at least as interesting to converse with as some people I know.

"The last wall I built was in the back of the house under the mesquite trees. I wanted to replicate the feeling of just standing in some of these canyons and looking at the old Anasazi ruins, especially in Cedar Creek and Sycamore and watching the shifting play of shadows on the walls as the sun arcs, at one with that feeling, completely immersed in it, emotionally sunk in, needing nothing more. It's a very psychotropic spot back there.

"Katie Lee, a songwriter and writer who took us on some of our greatest backcountry adventures, says most of us have lost our tentacles to the earth, but those of us who have spent a lot of time in those canyons and built walls, have not. The feeling is like that of looking at a great painting, El Greco's *View of Toledo* comes to mind, it sucks me in and keeps me there for hours, wrapped in that ineluctable modality of time, at utter peace with myself."

In 1993 a blowout occurred in a 100-foot wide by 75-foot section of an old hand-stacked wall built by the WPA in the 1930s on the highway that leads out of Jerome to Prescott. The building of the new wall was a technocrat's dream, beginning with seismic studies because it was very close to the large Verde fault. Fifteen-foot long I-beams were pounded in front of the wall and horizontally under the road. Railroad ties were placed between the I-beams and the wall filled with millions of tons of gravel. Concrete trucks with 40-foot flex snouts poured some 35 cubic yards of concrete for its face. The concrete isn't visible because ADOT faced it with rocks to resemble the adjacent massive hand-stacked retaining wall that still stood. Photo by Bob Swanson, www.SwansonImages.com

Eleven
Crossroads of Change:
The Deaths of Ferne Goldman
and Father John

When my husband and I arrived in Jerome late in 1979, stories about Father John and Ferne Goldman dominated conversations.

Father John was the Basque priest who had held Mass in the Holy Family Catholic Church since 1927. He embodied the piety and devotion of the Catholic mining community that was slowly disappearing.

Ferne was the gypsy godmother of the hippie wayfarers that were drawn to this abandoned mining town. She was part of the dreams and hopes of the new Jerome whose future was only beginning to be defined.

Their deaths marked a crossroads of change in Jerome. Within two decades, Jerome would pass from being a dilapidated town on the side of a mountain to a wealthy art and history Mecca.

Ferne Goldman

Ferne's name cropped up at least two or three times a day.

"This is one of Ferne's patchwork vests of flowers and butterflies. Here's the secret pocket near my underarm where I carry my pot and pipe."

"When Jasmina was born, Fernie gave me a whole wardrobe she had made of velvets, laces, and satins."

"Ferne ends her dinner parties by bringing out the vacuum cleaner and turning it on. People leave in a hurry."

"I made the crochet piece for the Ferne blouse you are wearing," said Roberta Westcott's mom.

Everyone talked about Ferne's beauty and big heart, her inclusion of people without judgment. She was a woman without an exclusionary heart. Many women and men claimed to have been her lover.

I could not wait to meet her. It seemed as though she hovered unseen around every corner I turned.

The picture that formed in my mind was that of a thin, young beauty, hair that framed an oval face, perfectly formed breasts, and shapely legs that loved to pirouette on roller skates.

No one mentioned that Ferne weighed over three hundred pounds. When I found out, it made me even more curious to meet her. The overweight people I knew were never called beautiful.

Finally, I asked one of my new friends, "When am I going to meet Ferne?" Shock gripped his face. "She died six months ago," he finally said. "She's only alive in people's hearts."

The Knitter of Hearts

It was not only the hippies that loved Ferne. She attracted people like bees to honey. They were embraced by Ferne's warmth. She was an icon of the period in Jerome that was like a magical spring idyll—love and frolic, flowers and butterflies, communal feasts, and music and dancing.

She was an extraordinary seamstress and opened The Downhill Trading Company under the Central Hotel. She helped to organize Emiliano's where they sold furniture, crafts, jewelry, and beadwork made by Jerome artisans.

No one could really describe Ferne's extraordinary charisma although everyone spoke of it. Even Katie Lee, who, at the age of sixty, mixed flamboyant charisma and eloquence, was flummoxed. The best she came up with was, "It was noth-

Ferne Goldman in her Jerome shop. Courtesy Jerome Historical Society (J-1990-459-191).

ing you could put your finger on, you just knew. Ferne was a great trader, not a horse trader where something would be missing, or the thing you bought just was not in good condition, and she never seemed to do anything for cash. She was a New York Jew and although she was fat, she was very feminine. She knew how a big person should dress, colorful skirts and a blouse that would show her cleavage. She had great cleavage."

Ferne and Gary Shapiro

Ferne moved to Jerome in 1972, from Tempe, Arizona, where she had a shop called Leather and Lace. Ferne lived at Gary Shapiro's house and was the great love of his life. Gary was the town plumber. When Gary arrived with his tools and cassette player, we knew to disappear. The first thing he did was to put on an opera and turn it up loud so the music would drown out his curses as he tried to unscrew pipes or clean out sewer lines.

One day, I trudged up to Gary's house to interview him. His house was up a dirt road near the bottom of the Gulch. It looked like a giant nest perched on wood stilts. There was a small forest of forty or fifty apricot, quince, pear, apple, black walnut, and oak trees; honeysuckle, roses by the dozens, blackberries, orange trumpet flowers, ivy, and the purple flowers of vinca. Birds sang and hundreds of bees buzzed and pollinated.

This little oasis contrasted with the rest of the barren hillside that contained mine tailings, remnants of shacks, hundreds of rusted tin cans, broken pipes, and bedsprings.

There was a crapper on the porch (though not quite an outhouse) and a refrigerator on the patio. Inside, Gary's house was suffused with Ferne. The first thing I noticed inside was the beautiful Tiffany-style lamp with agate slices embedded in the leaded glass shade and its intricate Moroccan base. Ferne had traded a king-size velvet patchwork quilt to the artist who made it at one of the early Whole Earth festivals.

Narrow shelves held jars full of seeds, herbs, beads, rocks, and pottery. There was a rug on the kitchen floor. There were two old iron burners for a stove, a sink with only cold water, chairs of mixed breeds, and the floors and walls tipped crazily in every direction, just like the town. There was not a straight line anywhere.

Gary showed me many pictures of Jerome. I saw photos of my new friends in their younger days, quite a few children, and many shots of Ferne. One showed her as she turned a goat on a spit at one of her feasts, and another showed her in one of her flowered vests with buffalo nickel buttons. Still another showed Ferne in the pose of a whore, dressed in a lacy black bodice to her hips, a garter belt held up black stockings, all arms and legs, soft contours, round cheeks, and big girlish smile.

Gary's Monologue about Ferne

"This was Ferne in her sluts-in-a-shack days. She and her friend Janis would wear negligees and hang out on the porch luring hitchhikers up to the house. Even though Ferne was fat, I always thought of her as petite. She had small hands and feet and wore bangles from her fingers to her elbows. She was a munchkin type, really quite cute, and she could be graceful and dainty on roller skates.

"She had a great dynamic spirit. Everyone remembers her for lavish Thanksgiving feasts for hundreds where we'd roast goats on spits. She loved children and would gather them up and drive them down the hill and into the magic of the creeks and pools of the Verde River or Sycamore Canyon. Before she came to Arizona, she taught school at the Haile Selassie School in Ethiopia.

"We were always traveling and wherever we went we traded patchwork quilts filled with butterflies and flowers, peyote buttons, ivory, and Slovakian beads. Ferne was an old-fashioned trader, a real wheeler-dealer. She opened The Downhill Trading Company, which had jewelry and clothes and crafts of all kinds. It really made the town quite famous at the time and it got written up in one of the newspapers.

"The year before she died, Ferne wanted to lose weight and began reading a book that taught her about the psychology of losing weight. She was taught to fix and focus her attention on what she ate and when, and in that paying of attention, she began to learn about the habits that contributed to her being fat, and she began to change them. She lost almost a hundred pounds.

"The December before she died, I gave Ferne a bike. The week before the bike accident, she and about eight friends had a bike race to Camp Verde and finished up at a feast in the Copper Kitchen over there. She won that race.

"Ferne knew that I was a homosexual when we got together. I lied my way all the way through high school about it and began to dislike living that lie. These days I tell people right off, because you want to know who your friends are. I never lied to her.

"She was the most moral and ethical person I knew, one without manipulation—a rare quality—and everyone knew it at once. She never took advantage of anyone.

"We loved each other very deeply. I've never really lived with anyone since."

Ferne's Bike Accident

You could coast all of the way to Clarkdale with your car in neutral, and many people in Jerome did that when they were short on gas and money. It was downhill, with only a few curves. Traffic had not yet grown to the long ribbons of cars, trucks, and motorcycles we have today. Bicycles went very fast.

It was probably the combination of Ferne's speed and that her bicycle hit the cattle guard wrong that caused her to fly over the handlebars.

Jeanne Moss told me she was the last person to see Ferne before the accident.

"I was riding in my car. Jasmina Henley was with me, she was only about five or six then, and we were on our way to the market. We passed Ferne on her bike near the old gas station down near the curve. Ferne waved. I remember exactly what she was wearing—babushka, mittens, sweats, down jacket. By the time I got down the hill and made the turn toward Cottonwood, the ambulance was already on its way up the hill."

From the moment that Ferne went to the emergency room, dozens of friends came down to hold vigil in the waiting room. Dr. Henry Kaldenbaugh was on duty and came out crying to tell them that she was in a coma.

"Ferne is brain dead, but her body is still pumping, so we can't declare her dead yet, but I want you all to be clear that she can't feel anything, her brain can't feel anything, technically she is dead."

Hundreds showed up for the memorial that was held in the Episcopal Church, which had become the center for the Jerome Historical Society. Richard Martin gave the eulogy. "I was crying the whole time," he said. "Everyone felt her spirit so strongly."

During the thirty years that I lived in Jerome, no one else's death was felt so strongly and so sadly. It was as though a sense of something more than just a hippie with a big heart had died. Her death marked the passing of a freehearted decade, something to be felt with nostalgia and longing.

And as time went on, many linked her death and that of Father John as the beginning of the major changes that now define contemporary Jerome.

Father John

Father John's full name was Juan Atucha Gorostiaga. He was born in the Basque town of Legazpi, Spain, and he belonged to the Claretian order, which ministers to the spiritual needs of the poor.

Father John held formal Mass in the Holy Family Catholic Church for the six devoted parishioners that still lived in Jerome in 1979.

The windows of his church, painted with martyred saints, were gray relics of their once bright colors. The turquoise fleur-de-lis on the tin ceiling looked faded and dull. Candle wax was pooled on altar vestments. The musty odor of bat guano emanated from the church attic where hundreds of bats made their home. The rustle of the air from their wings was a silken breeze. The ghosts of thousands of devout parishioners that knelt before him to be baptized and married were like faint harmonies woven through his melodic Latin rituals.

Father John would sit on the steps of the brick and sandstone church in his cassock and black Spanish hat. The steep street, paved with worn limestone blocks, was often empty. His featherless chicken would cluck at food scraps on the sun porch and his three little dogs would nap. He was a scarecrow, withered into a cassock that was too big for him and he had become a cranky diabetic.

One day, a woman interrupted Father John's reveries. Her breasts, unfettered by bra, bounced under her thin blouse as she kicked at Father

Father John and one of his dogs. Glen Baisch Collection, courtesy Jerome Historical Society.

John's dogs that nipped at her long gauzy skirt. Suddenly, Father John's voice cut the air. He yelled that she had torn the toenails off one of his dogs and had stolen his mail. He said she was a serpent because she did not come to church, and he warned her about living with the ghosts in the houses on Company Hill.

"The houses are dead, the houses are dead," he shouted.

The hippie newcomers seemed like a weird dream to Father John. He met them everywhere—at the post office, on horses near his property outside of town, and as they strolled dreamily past his church. The intruders could not be chased away.

He found himself suspended between two realities—the Jerome of the old mining days, alive with money and bustle, and the new Jerome that was peopled with unkempt hippies—a surreal purgatory that gave him no peace.

Father John Loses Control of His Life

Glen Baisch, Roger Davis, and Richard Martin, three hippie newcomers, noticed that Father John had not been seen for several days. They could not recall him at the post office in his 1957 Ford Falcon or spitting invective from the church steps. No one had seen his dogs.

They decided to look for him in the church. As they stepped from the dark vestibule into the nave, a priest who stood sentinel halted them. Al-

Interior of the Catholic Church. Photos by Bob Swanson, www.SwansonImages.com

though they understood in a moment that the priest was a statue, it unnerved them. The statue was so lifelike that they continued to stare. The whitish face reminded them of the way people look after they have been embalmed.[66]

They noticed a "No Trespassing" sign on the table in front of the altar.

The faint yap of dogs directed them to a basement bedroom. They had to take the door off its hinges to enter. They were assaulted by the rubble of cardboard boxes, clothing, magazines, newspapers, books, tin cans full of money, and shoes, which was piled high and had toppled over. There were Mason jars full of urine everywhere and even though they had lids on, the room reeked of urine and an old man's decay. There were dozens of fruitcake tins under the bed.

The dogs nipped and tugged at their trousers. The men made their way toward the mattresses piled like a haphazard dome on a bed frame.

They did not see Father John right off, but they heard a wheezy grunt. Father John was wedged between the wall and the mattresses. Maybe he rolled off in his sleep and was too weak to climb out; maybe he suffered a small heart attack or stroke; maybe his body had gone to sleep. His green wool union suit was damp from where he pissed himself.

Glen and Richard lifted him to the bed. He felt like a rag doll. Barely conscious, Father John wheezed some incoherent words in several languages—rumor was he knew at least sixteen. Glen tried to give him some water and Richard went to find someone who spoke Spanish.

Suddenly, the room was full of cops, medics, and two of his faithful parishioners. The dark room was charged with pandemonium. When the medics placed Father John on the stretcher, he quivered and suddenly came to life. His eyes seemed to burst out of his head; he waved his arms and shouted in a horrible voice, *"Hospitale no! Hospitale no!"* He was so strong and wild that he had to be strapped down. He kept fighting and yelling, *"Hospitale no! Hospitale no!"*

He was no longer in control of his life.

Father John's Life is Stolen

The next morning, just before dawn, Father John's house mysteriously caught fire. By the time fire trucks arrived, all that was left were eight or nine iron woodstoves and a corrugated tin shed that was full of ladies shoes—right foot only. I once asked one of Father John's parishioners what he thought about those shoes. He looked me in the eye and said, "He was Basque and Basques have strange ways."

Fireman Jimmy Kinsella told me the house did not have electricity or gas, and he speculated that someone had to have started the fire. Not too long before Father John got wheeled away, Jimmy spoke with a guy (he never said who) who bought a few of Father John's antiques, not the tiger-striped oak piano, but some of the smaller antiques. Jimmy figured the man came back after they put Father John in the hospital, robbed the house and then set fire to it.

A few days later, Vince Henry caught two men as they came out of the church with grocery bags full of rolled up silver dollars and half dollars. The men got away but Henry took the money to Ron Ballatore, one of Jerome's policemen.

"It was the first time I knew for sure that Father John stashed away money in the church," said Ballatore. "When I'd meet him at the post office, he'd say, 'Ron they're stealing from me.' But never would he say that he had money in the place or even owning anything that was very valuable. I just thought he was losing it and couldn't take care of himself. By that time, he was ornery, obnoxious, stubborn, and paranoid."

That is how people in Jerome came to know that Father John never spent much of the money that his parishioners had given him. The police, the old parishioners, and some firemen hunted around and found silver coins in shoeboxes and fruitcake tins in his bedroom and in the walls. There were old bills stuffed into chinks in the walls and floorboards, under altar vestments, flattened in liturgical books, squirreled away in the ventilation system. It was the biggest live treasure hunt they had ever taken part in. "By the time we started looking, who knows how much was stolen," said Ballatore. "Inside the downstairs door, we found money all sacked up and ready to load. And who knows what might have been in the house that burned down."

Police recovered $8,000 in silver and antique coins. Ron said, "The paper money was shredded by rats, worthless. The diocese in Phoenix told us to give it to three of his loyal parishioners and ask that it be used to fix up the church. Three of the old-timers that had stayed behind when the mines closed showed up: Tony Lozano, Alfredo Guitterez, and Doc Joe Pecharich. What happened to it after that I don't know. I do know that Tony spent years repairing that church pretty much on his own."

Stories of the theft of church money and antiques from the home that burned circulated for many years after Father John died. By the time I moved to Jerome in 1979, people told me that $75,000 and maybe even $125,000 had been stolen, and they whispered the names of people that might have stolen it or set fire to the house. One construction worker swore that he saw silver certificates in the safe of a house he was remodeling. He would not say whose house. He said there were probably many thieves.

Jimmy, the fireman who helped find and collect the money in the church, told me that some months afterward, someone bought breakfast for two friends and paid for it with eighteen one-dollar bills, all dated 1957. When Jimmy came in a few hours later, the waitress brought the bills to him.

"Jimmy, have you ever seen anything that looks like this?"

Jimmy pulled out a twenty and bought them from her. He kept them in a drawer at his house and said they smelled just like the shoeboxes and fruitcake tins full of money that he had found in the church.

In 2011, I was surprised with this confession of stealing from the church by someone nobody had previously associated with it. He showed me some of the certificates that he had saved as souvenirs.

"Months after Father John died, three of us went up to the church at three A.M. There was nobody around. We broke into the basement to look for old bottles. We poked around with flashlights, and I spotted an old wine keg covered with rat shit and a shredded burlap bag. When we tried to lift the keg, the bottom fell out and so did some fruitcake tins. I opened a tin and saw piles of lime green silver certificates. Suddenly, two cats were screeching and fighting: from the sound of it they were right near us, and then we heard a huge thunderclap. We got scared. We each picked up a fruit-cake tin and went running home. Mine contained exactly $7,777. Seven was always my lucky number. I bought two pounds of hash, a quarter ounce of cocaine, and an old Les Paul guitar. I sold the hash and bought eight pounds of marijuana. The profits got us through the year and the money circulated through the town."

Requiem for Father John

Andy Peterson was Father John's altar boy for seventeen years and was married in his church. Andy and his family lived in the Phelps Dodge office that sat on the knoll opposite the open pit just outside of town.

Andy loved Father John.

"He never refused to give a sacrament, a baptism, or a funeral because someone was too poor. One of the beautiful Selna daughters became a nun because of him; he taught her to play the pipe organ that's still in the church.

He baptized bar owner Jerry Vojnic's son when the priests in the valley wouldn't because they said Jerry hadn't been to mass often enough.

"He was the most wonderful priest and was known for his kindness. When he would say the gospel and say his sermon, everyone would pay attention. At every mass, he played the organ and sang beautifully. Afterward, he would have catechism for the children, show films, feed them lunches, and then blindfold them and let them try to hit the clay piñatas full of candies. There would be maybe forty, fifty kids."

When Andy found out that Father John was in the hospital in Cottonwood, he made a special trip to see him. The nurses told Andy that they could not get Father John to talk or eat; he was not responding to treatment and he would not look at anyone. Andy persuaded the nurse to let him go in.

"Right away I started talking Spanish to him and after a while Father John got some expressions on his face. I said, 'Father would you like me to sing for you?' and he said 'Si.' I sang *Venete Adoremus*, 'Come Let Us Adore Him.' When Father John sang that at Christmas, he used to hold the little Christ child for people to come and kiss Jesus' feet and then he'd wipe it off after each kiss. He had a little towel. While I was singing, he started smiling and nodding his head yes. When I finished, tears were pouring down my face. I was crying like a baby. The nurses told me he was peaceful after that. Just thinking about it makes my heart beat a little harder."

Father John died a few days after Andy's visit. The local newspaper printed no obituary.

A great blasphemy had been committed: theft from a priest because the love of money was an insatiable desire. And maybe, just maybe, that greed was a harbinger of events that brought Jerome to its knees in the 1980s and contributed to the new gold rush of tourism in the 1990s.

Twelve
A Vision of Jerome's Future

Matt Winkle, a Certified Planner from the Northern Arizona Council of Governments, was hired by the town of Jerome in 1977 to help volunteers develop a plan for the future of the town. At the first meeting, Matt said "If your town is going to die, you don't need planning and zoning or a plan; if it's not going to grow, you don't need a plan either. But if you think your town is going to grow, then a comprehensive plan, teamed with a planning and zoning ordinance, can provide the framework within which change may occur. You folks will have to decide your future."

Future was an odd concept in a town that was rapidly heading toward destruction. Although a great deal had been done to establish museums that heralded Jerome's history and to bring visitors to Jerome, there was little money to restore the rapidly decaying water and sewer systems and decrepit homes and buildings.

The goal for people in private residences was to make them livable, according to lifestyle. The condition of many homes was comparable to those on Company Hill. They needed far more repairs than there was time and money. The Jerome Historical Society used their scant funds to make interior spaces of commercial buildings usable when renters applied for them.

Although people were supposed to apply for construction permits, few did. And no one chased after anyone to ensure they did so. The informal and unwritten agreement seemed to be "Repair what you can." There were no ordinances, no design codes. At most, someone from the fire department would hold informal neighborhood inspections to ensure that electrical and heating systems were safe.

There were rumors that Kentucky Fried Chicken wanted to open up a restaurant in Jerome and that Knott's Berry Farm wanted to turn Jerome into a theme park. What was going to stop them from building truly ugly buildings?

Perhaps it was time to turn the negative—We don't want that! —into a positive to determine what people in Jerome did want and codify rules to accommodate that vision.

Codifying Jerome's Uncertain Future

More than two-dozen newcomers responded to the need to plan for an uncertain future.[67]

All had migrated to Jerome within the decade and they represented a cross-section of the new community. Two were architects; one was a geologist; some were artists and writers; some were hippies. Most of them were not yet thirty years old, but four were in their sixties. Many would hold positions on future Town Councils and boards.

They were very different from the austere group that formed the Jerome Historical Society. They were not marooned and they were not conservative. They chose to move to Jerome because they liked the freewheeling, quirky lifestyles of what many termed "their tribe"—like people, with like minds that created fresh lives. What they did have in common with the old-timers was that they strongly felt they had a stake in determining Jerome's future and a sense of unity whose commonality was a love for the town. It may have been a new-found love, but it was driven by a lot of heady, positive energy.

It was perhaps the first time that anyone on the committee to plan Jerome's future had direct experience in drafting plans and laws. What overcame their dislike of laws, rules, bureaucracy, and authority—stuff that many of them had run from—was the opportunity to create ordinances that reflected their lifestyle and philosophy.

Richard Martin in his 1949 Studebaker pickup, circa 1979. Photographer unknown, courtesy Richard Martin collection.

Richard Martin, the leader of this volunteer committee, called it "The great Jerome experiment to see if we could bend legislation to make sure 'goodness' pervades for all time, and incidentally, at the same time establish the dreamed-of hippie toe-hold on the cliff of self-government."[68]

The committee took the town's designation as a National Historic Landmark and its growing artist community very seriously. What standards should be imposed for safe and orderly restoration of existing buildings to maintain their historic nature? What standards should be applied for new buildings and homes? How was the town going to provide for an influx of tourists? If the town grew in population, how much growth was desirable? How many new people could the sewer system support? What kind of businesses did the town want to attract? These were not simple questions, and they led the committee down unexpected paths.

They met every other week for over two years to answer them. They wrote a comprehensive plan that outlined goals for the future of Jerome and drafted zoning and design ordinances. It was direct democracy at its finest.

First they did their homework. They listed existing businesses in Jerome and the availability of commercial rentals and empty lots that could hold new businesses. They photographed the residences in Jerome and researched the history of when they were built. They looked at architectural characteristics that defined neighborhoods, the commonalities of some of the large public buildings, such as the Clark Street School, the Little Daisy Hotel, the hospital (that dominated views from many vantage points), and the commercial buildings. They examined the potential of uptown Jerome to attract and serve tourists and provide for overnight stays and parking. They looked at the buildings that could accommodate new businesses and asked what kind of businesses they wanted to attract. They looked at empty lots and asked what might curb new commercial buildings from encroaching on neighborhoods.

The Grand Hotel today. Photo by Finetooth, from Wikimedia GNU Free Documentation License.

The hospital as it looked in 1985, before being bought from Phelps Dodge and restored as The Grand Hotel. Restoration required that the owners conform to building and fire safety codes. Photo by Bob Swanson, www. SwansonImages.com

119

They examined architectural characteristics. What they found was that Jerome had no defined architectural heritage. What homes and buildings had in common was that all of them, with only a few exceptions, were built prior to 1953 to accommodate the needs of a mining city. Many neighborhoods differed in style and usage. The Victorian-like homes on Company Hill, built for management by United Verde, differed from homes in the Mexican barrios and from those in the neighborhoods that mixed boarding houses and triplexes with single-family homes.

They found that the number of new buildings that could be accommodated within Jerome's city limits was limited: the whole town occupied about a square mile of real estate. Growth was also limited outside of town because most of the land was still owned by mining companies. Crowding was the norm in certain neighborhoods. And with the new era came ownership of cars, sometimes more than one per family. Some neighborhoods experienced crowding of a new kind—no place to park.

The research kept leading to more questions. "We philosophized and pontificated," Richard Martin said, remembering those sessions. "The ideas ranged from brilliant to annoying; esoteric to greedy; practical to absurd. Some of the more senior in the group snoozed their way through many a session, while a few of the more excitable nearly exploded in frustration."

At the heart of the discussion was how the town could plan for orderly growth supported by infrastructure, preserve common architectural elements in discrete neighborhoods, and the limitations of available parking areas.

The New Ordinances

The committee divided Jerome into specific zones—commercial, residential, agricultural, light industrial—which helped define the types of businesses and buildings that would be allowed in each one.

They defined a range of new businesses that were desired, some to accommodate the burgeoning tourist business (more places to stay overnight), others to accommodate the needs of residents (small grocery store, home businesses), still others to provide for economic diversity. No one desired a town that would be wholly dependent on tourism.

They looked at the potential for newcomers and estimated that a population of twelve hundred would be the upper limit that would be desirable and practical, given the built-in limitations of parking, available building lots, and town limits.

The remains of the brick "cribs," home of Jerome's ladies of the night during Jerome's mining heydays. The cribs were taken down by Michael Farkas, former co-owner of the shop called Skyfire, to gain access to the back of the building without permission from the Design and Review board. The board asked him to save the bricks and at least rebuild the façade, but he never did. The bricks were neatly stacked, then they slowly disappeared. As Jane Moore commented, it was a "crime." Photo by Gary Romig.

But in 1977 newcomers meant permanent residents. No one imagined that growth would mean that countless tourists would be in Jerome on any given day. And no one thought about the impact that would have on the infrastructure of the town and the lifestyle of its residents. Although an increase of tourism was desired, no one envisioned that Jerome would, within two decades, draw more than a million visitors a year.

Nor did anyone envision a time when the population might dip below 400 and leave a shrunken pool of people to fill the many volunteer jobs that ran the town: the historical society, fire department, chamber

Arizona Copper Camp Hotel circa 1953 on upper Highway 89A. The building began to deteriorate and was boarded up. Today it is being meticulously restored according to Jerome's codes. Courtesy Richard Martin.

of commerce, and humane society, among others. They did not think about what would happen if a great many homes were rented as vacation rentals to an itinerant population that would not care about their impact on the town's infrastructure.

The committee examined what design criteria could be applied toward restoration and new buildings. Two principles were chosen. First, restoration of existing commercial and residential buildings must maintain their original outward structure and appearance, as much as they could within modern safety and fire codes. As an example, the Connor Hotel on Main Street could not add another two stories. New homes were to reflect the character and "rhythm" of the neighborhood. An example was that you could not put in large picture windows in a neighborhood that never had them.

Once the ordinances were drafted, the committee set up three boards to administer them: Planning and Zoning; Design Review; and a three-person Board of Adjustments to reconcile differences between the boards and applicants.

The town of Jerome adopted the Comprehensive Plan and Historic Preservation Survey and new ordinances in 1981. They were not perfect documents, but they were good blueprints. They reflected the hopes of the committee for Jerome to continue to work for historic preservation and the arts, growth of new business, and be a pleasant community to live in.

Compliance, the Sticky Wicket

Few people on the drafting committees foresaw the difficulties of enforcing the ordinances. What was thought to be the common good would conflict with the self-interest of people that wanted to make money. The conflict between individual freedom and property rights versus the constraints of ordinances would rear its ugly head as Jerome headed into its boomtown years.

The town of Jerome depended on voluntary compliance for the first few years. The town could not afford a full-time zoning administrator or a full-time building inspector. Most businesses complied and dutifully brought plans for restoration or new buildings to be reviewed by the Design Review and Planning and Zoning boards because they were directly in the public eye. Included were the restoration of such Main Street buildings as the Boyd Hotel, the Sullivan Apartments, Pay 'n Takit, Mine Museum building, Connor Hotel, Skyfire, the New State Motor building, and upper

Main Street buildings. New commercial buildings included Pura Vida Gallery, Aurum, Made in Jerome Pottery, Jerome Gallery, Raku Gallery and glass studio, and the Queens Neighbor Art Gallery. They were visible signs that art was a big draw for tourists.

As new buildings came on line and tourism increased, the pressure for providing more uptown parking grew, and with it, a desire for ordinances that required new builders to provide parking. Although committees formed and tried to draft parking ordinances, the issues were onerous, complicated, and divisive, and not a whole lot came of them.

Residence owners continued to repair and restore as money and time was available. As demand for rentals and overnight stays increased, residential owners began to remodel their homes to accommodate that need, often

The Verdugo House at the top of the Gulch circa 1985. By the time Richard Martin bought the home in 2011, it had further deteriorated. In 2014, restoration led by Chuck Runyon is very nearly completed. Building codes that required expensive engineering studies for the new foundation were a major expense. Photo by Bob Swanson, www. SwansonImages.com

without applying for permits or supplying parking. Neighborhood squabbles over parking places became increasingly common.

Noncompliance was not a secret, especially to members of the Town Council and Planning and Zoning and Design Review boards. They watched their neighbors ignore the ordinances and talked amongst each other about what to do. The inequality of how standards were applied, one for residential, one for commercial, and the fact that some of those who built illegally were friends, and even family, weighed heavily on their consciences. Nobody wanted to play the rat. "Isn't that what you get when a town full of rebels also makes the laws," said my husband Walter, who was elected to the Jerome Town Council in the nineties.

Finally, one member of the council said, "We need a dragon at the gates, someone willing to be a strong planning and zoning enforcer." A person who fit that bill was hired and instructed about protocols. When anyone brought an illegality to her attention, she would write a series of letters, asking them for compliance. After that, it was threaten a lawsuit time.

This worked to some degree until a newcomer wanted to build a home that was larger, grander, and definitely noncompliant to any design criteria in the neighborhood where it would be. The town sued and did not prevail. It would not be the first time.

As the town began to pay more attention to how to enforce their ordinances, they spent more money each year on lawyers for advice. It did not take long, however, for some people to realize that they had more money to sue than the town did to defend.

It is difficult to accommodate freedom and individualism within the constraints of law and ordinance. Money almost always won.

Thirteen
Jerome's Guerilla Marijuana Industry

Six months after I moved to Jerome, I bartered for office space on the fourth floor of the Clark Street School with a software designer who had asked me to write a manual for an Apple computer database system that he designed. It was my first writing job in Jerome. He said I could use the office to offer my services as a writer-for-hire to others.

One day, James Faernstrom, a 1970s newcomer, asked me to edit a guerilla gardening manual. He got right down to business.

"I'm writing a practical step-by-step guide to anyone who wants to grow the best bud they've ever smoked and make a pot of money."

"How big a garden are we talking about?" I asked.

"A one-thousand plant garden grown in the mountains behind Jerome."

I did not gasp, but I wanted to. It was the first time I had heard about the Jeromans that were growing pot in large gardens.

He offered me $15 an hour.

I told him I'd think about it.

I found Faernstrom to be smart, charming, arrogant, and boorish. I was astounded at the trust he placed in me. Had I just become an instant part of some magic inner circle? I knew I had been checked out to some degree, but I was surprised at how easily someone revealed the details of his outlaw industry just because I smoked pot, had worked in the music business, and made a few friends among Jerome hippies.

I checked him out. He was the managing editor of *The Verde Independent,* the local valley newspaper in 1972. He was fired the same year for his editorial that slammed Richard Nixon for being a crook. He moved to Jerome and worked as a bartender in the Spirit Room.

I found out he had a self-destructive and manic side, perhaps even a bipolar personality. "Equally charismatic and ugly," one friend said. Another told me James had a weird form of epilepsy, sometimes triggered after days of drinking, which would result in him beating up his girlfriends or getting into fights at the bar. Still another told me he was nicknamed "Spittin' Jim" because he would spit on people when he wanted to fight and could claim self-defense when he hit them back. One friend remembers him not stoned and not drunk but in a melancholy state one evening. He poked his forehead with a small bottle, over and over, until the indentations swelled and blood poured down his face.

Everyone agreed that he was the best pot grower in the state.

The high quality of Jerome pot was a source of great pride in the community. At many parties when the joints were passed around, someone always mentioned an article in *High Times* that was written during the 1970s, which praised the high quality of resinous *indica* grown in Jerome.

Although I was tempted to learn about this industry first-hand, I was more than a little paranoid. Even though most of my new friends, including many non-hippies, smoked pot and took LSD, peyote, and other psychedelics in copious amounts, growing pot was illegal. But there was no secrecy or paranoia about it in Jerome. This devil-may-care approach to life was part of the town's attraction for many of us.

When Faernstrom came to the office again, I admitted my paranoia. "Aren't you afraid of being busted?"

Author Diane Sward Rapaport (r) in her office at the old elementary school in the late 1980s. Susan Antman Kinsella, Diane's assistant for many years, is seated at the left. Photographer unknown, courtesy Diane Rapaport collection.

"You don't have to be paranoid if you disguise the garden the way we do," he said. "I'm not gloating, but almost everyone else has been ripped off. You could walk through our garden and be almost halfway through before you notice one plant. Just to walk through the garden when you know where all the plants are takes an hour. And a lot of climbing."

"How do you pull it off?"

"You make sure the garden is far away from water and locate it in the most uninviting and rugged terrain. Forget flat areas. The water source should be as much as a half-mile to a mile away and you need to dig a trench and bury the lines to the pot. You need to plant seeds in five-gallon buckets, space them at least twenty feet from each other, set them right next to indigenous trees and bushes, such as thick growths of Manzanita and cat-claw. When fully grown, the ideal height of each plant should be no more than four feet. You put netting over them so that if someone looks down from an airplane they wouldn't notice anything peculiar.

"You have to set the drip and feed lines on timers, so the garden is virtually self-maintaining, and workers don't have to etch a path to it. The heavy work, such as trenching, digging, laying underground water lines and drip systems, and carrying large amounts of five-gallon buckets should happen when you can be virtually guaranteed that nobody is up on that mountain. Thanksgiving Eve, New Year's Eve, Christmas Eve, and Easter Day are best. You need to do everything the hard way. If you do, you can expect freedom from the paranoia of being ripped off."

It sounded like he knew what he was talking about. In my mind, it all added up to a lot of very hard work.

I asked him about the business of running a garden that size. "I have a few partners and we make the key decisions, but basically we run it as an old-fashioned garden cooperative where everyone shares in the profits and the work. We don't give anyone a chance to argue about how we go about the work. If you were to tell your workers ahead of time that you were forming a cooperative, none of the work would get done, we'd end up in endless discussions. The beauty of this system is that everyone participates cooperatively, but the decisions are made by the partners ahead of time."

He handed me some pages that included some of the information he just told me and asked me to tell him what I thought. I was not sure how much more I wanted to know, but the fact is, I loved being on the inside of this industry. It gave me insight into how a part of Jerome ticked. I was a writer who was handed buckets of information without having to scrape very deeply.

Harvest Parties

The most communal activity of Faernstrom's business occurred during harvest, when the plants were picked, packed out from their remote locations, stacked, and dried properly. Then they were manicured, and the leaves and stems were removed. What was left was lovely, perfect, aromatic *indica* bud. "Maybe there's a little more money in leaving the shake on, but there is a pride factor in showing customers superior pot," Faernstrom told me.

"You need a cadre of loyal, trustworthy, dope-smoking friends. You shouldn't manicure at your residence or any of your partners. You need to rent other places. You should have bail money stashed with somebody to cover most or all of the people you will involve should any flukes happen.

"Trimming is the most boring work in the world. It's fun for maybe an hour or two, but nobody in their right mind would want to keep doing it unless you keep having it be fun *and* rewarding. We catered meals every night. Gave everyone all the booze they could drink, all the smoke they could smoke, and other treats.

"And after all the pot was distributed, we threw the hell of a biggest party we could for the people who helped, for any fellow growers we know, and asked all of them to help us out again next year, and prayed for everybody."

He was full of himself and fascinating at the same time, full of idealism and bluster. He espoused to some high principles.

"You can't buy loyalty. You can only reward it.

"The only way to avoid envy is not to be greedy.

"Ignorance and laziness are the only other two things that will blow your trip."

It was the rap of a guy who had an overblown sense of belief in the values of love, peace, and good vibes and making a lot of money at the same time. He was no different than a lot of people I had met and worked with in the music industry.

Although Faernstrom made a few more trips up to my office, the project drifted. I never knew whether he finished his manual. I did not see him a whole lot.

A few years later, I set up an advertising agency in Jerome. One day, Faernstrom walked in and wanted my partner and me to design a graphics package of a new business, "Stay Snug." He and one of his partners in the garden business invested some of their profits and invented an ingenious method of keeping waterbed sheets in place by using large garters. We tried them on our waterbed sheets, which had never stayed in place for even one night. With Stay Snug, they stayed in place until we needed to wash them. We made a bunch of Stay Snug packages, and Faernstrom and his partner took them to Las Vegas for a big gift show.

"What happened?" I asked when he returned. "We had so much fun partying, we never quite made it to the gift show." His friends told me he and his partner got very drunk the night before and passed out. That same year, the pot gardens had a bonanza harvest.

Jerome's Underground Economy

I soon learned that Faernstrom was not the only grower. The knowledge was not difficult to come by. If you lived in Jerome, you were trusted to remain close-lipped. Being close-lipped, however, did not mean that I did not ask questions when the subject of pot growing came up.

That is how I came to know others who had equally elaborate theories about how to disguise the fields, tap into water lines, put in sophisticated irrigation and fertilizer systems, and make a profit. There were many small growers that cultivated up to fifty plants and others that grew a hundred to five hundred plants in the wild mountains and canyons in the wilderness areas of Jerome and the Verde Valley.

Pot was Jerome's first major cottage industry. It generated enough to spread pot and money to a lot of people at a time when capital infusion was sorely needed. Jobs were scant. One estimate calculated that one twelve-foot plant or one four-foot bush, carefully cultivated would yield half a pound of manicured bud.

Faernstrom's estimate was more conservative. He figured that a hundred plants would yield thirty-eight pounds of manicured bud, priced at that time around $2,000 a pound.

I ran the math in my head. If there were at least one thousand plants scattered throughout the mountains that yielded 380 pounds of manicured bud, it added up to over half a million dollars worth of pot annually. The profits were spread throughout Jerome.

Pot was the first viable business to help rescue Jerome financially and move it toward restoration. Everyone had a story to tell me about how pot gardens helped business in Jerome, and how it benefited many people that did not smoke pot. The underground economy offered jobs that helped people buy construction tools and supplies to rebuild their homes. Jewelers used the money for equipment. Small business owners bought computers.

Money circulated in bars, restaurants, and shops. Retaining walls got built and homes became more livable.

"Money has no value at all until it changes hands," my friend Mimi Currier said. "It is not a commodity; it is a means of exchange. In Jerome, cash from the pot business changed hands at least ten times. Think of it this way. Someone has two ten-dollar bills. The first stays in a pocket and has zero value. The other goes through ten exchanges before it leaves town and has added $100 to the town's wealth."

How Secret Were These Gardens?

Eventually, the guerilla industry became an open secret to most that lived in Jerome.

"When I was working to fix leaks on the pipelines, I'd follow the trail of a leak so I could fix it," said Robert Sandoval. Robert was pretty çlose-lipped, or so he told me in an interview conducted in 2011. "Once I found fourteen gunny sacks full of plants and turned them over to the cops. The county guys came in and made them disappear. Another time I found a gallon full of seed and blew it away with a shotgun. But when I did fire inspections in the early seventies, if I saw pot or pipes in plain sight, I'd just mind my own business."

Duke Cannell was startled by pit bulls while he was riding his horse on Mingus Mountain. "I used to help him repair water lines, so Duke asked me what that was all about," his hippie friend Richard Martin said. "How was I supposed to answer? That I knew the dogs were probably guarding someone's pot field?"

A geologist told me he ran into one of those gardens while doing exploration drilling on Mingus. "I went to the mayor [by then a hippie] and said, 'In the next few months, I'm going to be leading bunches of geologists on tours up on the mountain; I'm not sure you want them stumbling into these gardens. You might want to put the word out.'"

A town crewman told me, "Walking the water lines to check for leaks was part of my job. One day, I came home and said to my brother, 'I saw these hoses sticking out from the water lines and then they went underground. What is that all about?' 'You never saw them,' my brother said. 'Forget about them and don't mention them to anyone.' I had no idea what he was talking about. A few months later, my brother and I went hiking up on the mountain and at one point he put a blindfold on me, and we walked about ten minutes more. When he took the blindfold off, we were in a marijuana forest. I saw plants no bigger than bushes strung out along the ground under mesquite trees, camouflaged from the air with net canopies artfully placed. If you didn't look too closely, you might not know what you were looking at. That was my initiation into the underground economy in Jerome. All I knew up to that point was that joints never stopped being pulled out and passed around. There was never any scarcity."

Trouble Brews

The communal business of pot gardens, albeit illegal, grew into a full-scale enterprise by 1982. At least half a dozen gardens produced between fifty and two hundred plants each, and some even more, on Mingus Mountain, in the remote areas of the Sycamore and Clear Creek wildernesses, and at Apache Lake. Most gardens were accessible only after driving five to ten miles on ragged dirt roads and hiking cross-country from there. There were no clear routes. No hiking trails. The country was steep, rocky, and dense with thorny acacia and cactus.

Marijuana from Jerome's guerilla gardens in the mountains outside of Jerome, one of the major industries that helped create Jerome's economic recovery. Photo by Michael Thompson.

Although pot cultivation was Jerome's inside secret, the growth of this business meant that new partners with money were drawn into the enterprise, and people from outside of Jerome were brought in as distributors and sellers. Not all were of savory character.

Members of some of Phoenix's more violent motorcycle gangs began to show up in Jerome. They drank beer with some of the growers and then disappeared to share more dangerous and addictive drugs. Heroin, cocaine, and meth were seen frequently, and among the users were the growers of the large gardens and their friends.

Rifts among the growers and distributors became common, some of them aired in the bars. Partners argued about how to split the profits; how to split the workloads; how big to grow the business; how many gardens the forests could sustain; and who was to have power and control.

The situation was rife with the probabilities of a bust.

The Bust at the Bamboo Corral

Ironically, the first police raid was not one of the large wilderness gardens, but one cultivated behind a home on Highway 89A in the middle of Jerome. The year was 1983.

Its discovery was due to reports made to the police by three self-proclaimed members of Jerome's ethics police—Steve Stevenson, Don Campbell, and Joe Marini—who wanted to get rid of dope-smoking hippies. One lived within half a block of that garden, and the rich odor of ripening pot plants would waft into his yard. They started investigating, and, sure enough, as they looked down from a nearby pathway they could see pot plants peeking out of a thick bamboo corral.

First, an Arizona Department of Public Safety (DPS) plane buzzed by low and loud. Soon afterward police arrested Glen Baisch and his girlfriend, then ripped up the plants and shoved them into the trunks of their cars.

The shocker was the one-inch newspaper headline in *The Verde Independent,* the local area newspaper, which focused not on the grower's arrest, but on accusations made by the self-proclaimed vigilantes about the chief of police: "Chief Accused in Drug Trafficking."[69]

The article quoted their suppositions: "Jerome residents have accused Jerome's police chief of ignoring a massive drug trafficking problem in the tiny community." "One of them said he's got a loaded gun in every room to protect himself from drug dealers who have threatened to kill him ... They requested anonymity because 'it's only a matter of time before the killing starts ...'"

The chief of police had not been arrested during the raid.

Afterward, the vigilantes wrote jubilant letters to the editor. Stevenson commended the paper for "having the guts and integrity to print the truth regarding the circumstances we have been living under in Jerome ... Let's all serve notice to the drug dealers. We will not tolerate them destroying the lives of our young people and the future of our community." Campbell wrote that older people were "afraid to even talk about it with their closest friends."[70] Marini commended the paper for its "courageous and truthful reporting ... I knew it was only a matter of time before someone wrote the truth about this town."[71]

Others wrote letters that condemned the newspaper and the vigilantes. The letters accused the paper of inept, tacky, misleading, biased, and shockingly sensationalist rubbish and yellow journalism. "Only a couple of stupid old fools would be capable of dreaming up the kind of crap *The Verde Independent* printed," said another.

The crap included a mistake in the number of plants that were confiscated. The initial article said that police ripped up 473 plants; the next week, however, the paper issued its correction: 87 plants.

Baisch pled guilty to a felony charge of possession of marijuana. He was placed on three years probation, fined $1,370, ordered to serve one hundred hours of community service work, and was sentenced to fourteen days in Yavapai County Jail. His girlfriend pled guilty to a misdemeanor for possession, was placed on probation for two years, ordered to perform fifty hours of community service, and serve two days in jail.

Baisch was not lazy, but he was naive and greedy, and never seemed to learn from his mistakes. A few years later he was arrested for selling drugs to teens. Rather than face jail time, he committed suicide.

Jesus and the Marijuana Leaf Crown

One day in 1982, Terry Molloy looked toward the Holy Family Catholic Church from his perch on the roof of the old fire station on Main Street, which he was repairing. What he saw astounded him. Papa Lozano appeared to be sawing the breasts off a wooden mannequin.

A few days later, Terry strolled up Company Hill Road and recognized the mannequin in the backyard of the church. It had become transformed into a life-size statue of Jesus Christ, nailed to a crude wooden cross. He wore a crude skirt and red paint

The statues of Jesus and the Thieves that Papa Lozano carved from mannequins. Photo by Diane Rapaport.

Statue of Jesus with marijuana leaf. Photo by Diane Rapaport.

was splattered on his wrists, fingers, and knees. Beside him were two more mannequins, equally bloodied with paint, transformed into Jesus' two thieves.

I went to the church one day and asked Papa Lozano why he had done this. He told me he made the statues as a way of thanking God for answering his prayers to cure his daughter. She had injured her back after falling down some stairs. When the doctors could do nothing for her, Lozano prayed to God to make her well. Her cure was miraculous. Lozano bought the mannequins from Goodwill for fifteen dollars each and created his tribute to God.

The night after *The Verde Independent* published its sensational headline that accused the chief of police of collusion to keep quiet about pot cultivation in Jerome, three men stole into the churchyard. One propped a ladder on the shoulders of the bloody replica of Jesus Christ. Another climbed up and nailed a new crown at the top of Jesus' cross: a large wooden marijuana leaf that was painted a flamboyant green. Another nailed a big sign with the last name of the chief of police on its stomach.

The sign was removed by morning. The marijuana leaf stayed on the top of Jesus' cross for six weeks. Although Papa Lozano came to the church every day to work on its restoration, either he never noticed it or chose to ignore it.

It was not an act of blasphemy against the church. It was retaliation against the hypocrisy of the newspaper, cops, and vigilantes; and a flagrant defiance against those that condemned pot smoking.

1984: The Green Flower Gardens

Stupidity and arrogance led to a second bust in Jerome in 1984. The sale of hard drugs to teens caused the FBI to raid a methamphetamine lab owned by Robert Amick, a Jerome newcomer, owner of Green Flower Gardens and Laboratory. Also arrested in conjunction with the laboratory were five members of the Dirty Dozen motorcycle gang.[72]

Those arrests should have acted as warnings that the police had a spotlight on Jerome. Instead, the drug business grew larger, rifts between partners more vocal, and visits by motorcycle gangs more regular.

The Snitch

On a foggy morning on Friday, October 11, 1985, a 6:30 A.M. phone call informed me that they had just seen six policemen hauling a friend of ours out of the house in handcuffs. The phone calls kept coming in. We knew it was a big bust.

Fifty state and federal narcotic agents arrested thirteen adults, including two Town Council members and one juvenile in Jerome. Eight were charged with "conspiracy to cultivate and distribute marijuana;" two with sale of marijuana; one with possession; one with four counts of sale of marijuana; and one with two counts of sale, as well as conspiracy. The same raid netted eight people in Cottonwood and Clarkdale.

Jerome's chief of police was arrested on the following Monday and charged with five felony counts of hindering prosecution (he was away on business the day of the raid). Two other Jerome citizens were arrested, one for allegedly "aiding in the production of marijuana," and one accused of cultivation.

Some that were arrested in Jerome reported that four to six policemen entered each home with guns drawn. One said the officers conducted themselves "like a bunch of pit bulls."[73] One person reported that when three policemen came to his house, they knocked and waited politely on the porch until he could restrain the dog and open the door. No guns were drawn. They let him read the warrant and did not search his house.

Police found only a scattering of marijuana in Jerome, except at two homes.

Those arrested were taken to a county annex in Cottonwood and then to the Yavapai County Jail in Prescott, where bail was set at $5,500 per person. As they talked among themselves, they noticed that one person who was close to them all was missing. They concluded that Faernstrom had become a snitch, a conclusion that was confirmed when their lawyers received the police reports.

The censure was loud and nasty. Faernstrom was a scumbag, a degenerate, a beater, and a greed monger. The Verde Valley Art Association gave him the sarcastic "Big Tipper" award. A mock gravestone placed inside the fence of the Gold King Mine read:

JAMES
FAERNSTROM
1945–1985
ON HIS FRIENDS
HE DID SNITCH
AND HE'S A DEAD
SON OF A BITCH

There were those that were angry enough to kill him, but James Faernstrom disappeared. While those that were arrested got out of jail on bail and hired lawyers, he was in protective custody, guarded by police.

A mock gravestone placed inside the fence of the Gold King Mine mocking James Faernstrom. Photo by Diane Sward Rapaport.

Welcome to Sin City

The day after the bust, local and national newspapers ran stories about the Jerome raid. It was a media blitz that was orchestrated to provide maximum shock. Although the raid was part of a nationwide crackdown against pot gardens, which the police called Delta Nine, the town of Jerome got the headlines. In the cops' minds, they had engineered a sensational bust that included town politicians and the chief of police.

The mythology of Jerome as an old ghost town was eclipsed by news of its wickedness. A dark side of Jerome was exposed that did not match the upbeat version of a town in renaissance.

The instant fallout of the publicity was that many Jerome people got phone calls from relatives and friends from all over the country. "What's going on in Jerome?" My brother and mother called with the usual platitudes about how horrible pot was and ended with, "I hope you weren't involved with *those* people."

"Dozens of clients called to get the inside story," said John McNerney, owner of Jerome Instrument Corporation. "I didn't know what to tell them."

For months, there was a long ribbon of traffic into Jerome from curiosity seekers—who knows what dirty secrets they expected to uncover. The cash registers were happy; the shopkeepers were glum and not too forthcoming when tourists asked prying questions. It proved that bad publicity draws more of a crowd than good publicity. Writer and songwriter Katie Lee, whose house was on the main highway, made a large sign to hang on her fence: "Welcome to Sin City. Now Go Home."

How a Man Turned Into a Rat

The discovery of the Clear Creek pot gardens was a fluke.

Two fishermen came down Clear Creek Canyon and saw a man pour gas into a generator and use it to power a pump to bring water to a ledge about 150 feet above the river. They spoke with the man who told them he was growing marijuana on a field over the ledge. One of the fishermen saw someone looking down from a ledge and asked the pot grower if they were going to be shot. The pot grower said that the man above was a working guy and a marathon runner who worked on aluminum siding in Phoenix. The fishermen reported the encounter to police.[74]

The police sent in surveillance teams.

In August 1985, police arrested Faernstrom at one of the Clear Creek gardens. Police discovered Faernstrom's prior felonies, which included burglary, parole violations, and a charge of unlawful flight from New York State police to avoid charges of assault with intent to murder, for which he was later caught and sentenced to two years in prison.[75]

Police pulled up 200 plants at one Clear Creek garden and 210 at another, according to investigation reports. They found 48 large plastic trashcans; an eight-horsepower gasoline generator, a water pump, hoses, climbing ropes, a tent, and camping gear. The generator was destroyed in place "due to the inability of available personnel to remove it from the site."[76]

No other arrests were made. Nor did any of his partners know that Faernstrom had been arrested.

Police cut a deal with Faernstrom to wear a voice transmission device (wire) and rat on his friends. He agreed because under the "three-strike" law in Arizona, a third felony conviction could have led to a mandatory lifetime sentence without parole.

Police gave him the code name "Lightning," because of a bolt of lightning that almost struck one of the agents that was camped out during surveillance. Subsequent reports of Lightning's activities identify him with the words "confidential informant."

Faernstrom met with police agents in Cottonwood from August through September a few times a week to discuss who he would meet that evening, and they would outfit him with the wire. He bought and sold small amounts of pot, discussed the gardens and fingered partners, friends, and a few people who were innocent bystanders, one of whom did not smoke pot at all. After Faernstrom's encounters, he would meet with his handlers, handwrite a report, and take off the wire. Police transcribed the transmissions. The reports were used to obtain search warrants.

One report detailed how Faernstrom met one of his friends in the Spirit Room and they went up to his room in the Connor Hotel. He told Faernstrom that he had harvested seven plants, showed him some of the dry bud, and quoted a price of $35 per quarter ounce. Faernstrom bought two buds for $10 and they discussed a new project for the future. When James returned to Cottonwood, he gave the pot to the agents.[77]

No one suspected that Faernstrom wore a wire. Nor did they imagine that a bust was imminent. After all, a few months had gone by since the pot growers reported that they had been surprised by two fishermen.

Others claimed, after the fact, that they noticed something "fishy." Jerry Vojnic, who owned Paul and Jerry's Saloon, said, "I felt suspicious about Faernstrom when he came in the bar every day with a different hair cut and his hair dyed different colors for two weeks running." Another said her dog was acting funny in his presence and it never had before.

"Now that I look back on it all, I see that he may have been dropping hints all over the place," said Jamie Peeples, one of Faernstrom's close friends. I asked him whether he was surprised to find that Faernstrom had snitched.

"I trusted Jim implicitly," Jamie said. "He had been such a good friend to me for so many years."

What Jamie did notice was growing volatility among the pot growers and friends.

"During the summer Jim lived out at the garden at Clear Creek so he could tend to the plants. One of his partners hiked in food and beer once a week. Sometime in July, maybe early August, Jim fell down a cliff and hurt his back. He went to his current girlfriend's house to recuperate, not able to move, not eating anything for a few days. I was a frequent visitor.

"Perhaps a week later, while Jim was still recuperating, obviously not out tending the fields, one of his partners barges into the apartment, salivating with anger, crazy drunk, knife in hand. Apparently during the period that Jim was not out camping at the fields, the plants got neglected and many of them wilted. 'Well, why weren't you out there?' Jim asked. One thing led to another and Jim was attacked. We pulled the guy off Jim and then called the cops, who came and threatened a restraining order.

"During this same period, pot plants were stolen from another Clear Creek garden that was not Jim's. The owner accused Jim of doing the stealing. Shortly afterward, Jim dyed his hair red and began to spew paranoia about being busted.

"Five days before the bust, he asked to borrow my stash of $500, saying that he just knew he was going to get busted and needed money to leave town with and that if I lent him the money, he promised to turn it into a quick thousand. So I let him have it. That evening, he told me he couldn't stand the thought of being put in prison and that if he was he'd kill himself with a knife first. Then he started sobbing. He was so sure he was going to get busted. It felt so strange to see him that way.

"And still I had no thought of any kind of betrayal or any premonition of a bust. I said to him, 'Let's go down to the bar and mellow out.' We had a few beers. And that was the last time I saw him. Four days later, the bust happened."

"Lightning" Bolts

Two months after the raid, on December 6, 1985, Faernstrom escaped protective custody from police. Apparently, he was afraid that there was a murder contract out against him. The cops said they felt "jilted" after doing such a good job of protecting him.[78]

His escape meant that he would not testify in court and would thereby avoid public disgrace and confrontations with his betrayed friends.

Although the raids revealed bagged marijuana and smoking paraphernalia at a few homes, the police needed Faernstrom to testify about his partners in the cultivation and distribution business. Even though police investigation reports indicated that police knew who the major growers and distributors were, no one else was arrested at the gardens.

Charges against eight people were dismissed outright. Fifteen defendants agreed to plea agreements in exchange for pleading guilty to misdemeanors for possession or sale. They were given jail terms ranging from one day to ninety days and a range of probation terms.

Ron Ballatore, the chief of police, agreed to a plea agreement in which he pled guilty to two counts of hindering prosecution. He was sentenced to one day in jail and two years of unsupervised probation and was disallowed from being a police officer again. The judge was influenced in his decision by over one hundred letters that commended the chief's ability to keep Jerome's violent crime rate low (one of the lowest in the United States), his service as an emergency medic, his personal accessibility, his warm optimism, and his love of the town and its people. Many letters praised him for his ability to mediate violent and abusive family situations.

Another defendant pled guilty to "False reporting to the Law" and was sentenced to one year of unsupervised probation. During the raid, when police officers asked where the entrance to the basement of her house was, she erroneously told them there was no entrance. "I was very scared and shaken." That she was held criminally accountable for words that arose from sheer terror and made to pay hefty legal fees to bring about a light sentence left her cynical and angry with the police and legal system.

Three people arrested, none from Jerome, received prison terms of two to six years for possession with intent to sell.

Jerome in Turmoil

The police raid was like an explosion. It shattered lives and caused immense turmoil. Those arrested were friends and neighbors. They were an integral part of the community. Six of them owned homes and had worked hard to restore them. They helped fill many volunteer positions. Our kids played with theirs. We smoked and partied with them; went camping and rafting.

The fallout wrapped us in collective mourning, guilt, and anger. We drew together, closed ranks, and began to pick up the pieces of lives that would never be the same.

As people made bail, everyone welcomed them back and helped them find lawyers and raise money. No one was ostracized or thought ill of. Many were quick to acknowledge the debt owed to the growers for having enabled them to start their businesses or learn their craft or fix up their homes.

Two of my friends and I formed "The Jerome Defense Fund" association and solicited donations for defendants to help them pay bail bond and legal fees. We held regular meetings, attended by many of those accused and their friends, and it became something between an information conduit and outlet for grief. We held a benefit dance, called Jail House Rock, with the help of 127 volunteers (twenty-seven of them musicians). The Main Street stores, without exception, and many artists made contributions for the large raffle that was held at the dance. We raised over $4,500 and split it among the defendants that needed money, including those who did not live in Jerome. Although it made a very small dent in what amounted to more than $75,000 in legal fees, the heart and solidarity behind it meant a great deal to the defendants.

The growers lost their cash crops and spent their emergency reserves on lawyers. The pot smokers lost access to good dope that was righteously grown, sold at a fair price, and was not sprayed with toxic herbicides, like paraquat, which was common in the pot that came from Mexico. The town lost the benefit of the easy cash from locals. Servers and bartenders saw a drop in tips almost immediately.

We lost a great policeman and two excellent members of the Town Council.

Jerome lost a cool business—the skating rink that opened in the high school gym in early 1980s. It was a popular place but after the bust, pastors of most of the churches in the Verde Valley ranted against sending children up to sin city. We felt sorry for the owner. It was a great use of the space.

Any number of us could have been arrested. We were all conspirators to the extent that we kept our mouths shut and did not complain about the unsavory characters that turned up with the addictive drugs. We may not have known about every garden, or their precise locations, but we kept our mouths shut. We were consumers of what we knew was illegal. We watched silently as the industry grew and dismissed our reservations with a cavalier optimism.

A lot of money had been spent on months of surveillance, on "handling" and guarding Faernstrom, and on the raid itself. The expenditure of so much money on a nonviolent crime that involved mostly nonviolent people was ill-spent in a county that was seeing large inroads of meth and the violent crimes it engendered.

Billy Lee Hicks, a Prescott lawyer who had also served as a prosecutor, told his Jerome defendants that it was well known in the Arizona law enforcement community that 90 percent of all violent crime in Arizona was alcohol induced. "Unfortunately," he said, "pot is illegal and you were an easy mark."

It was no surprise that many of us were openly defiant about having to deal with the fallout of a "crime" that few of us considered as such. We were a freewheeling community of dope smokers and close to arrogant about it.

The worst of the fallout was that the bond of trust among friends had been broken.

Faernstrom was part of a band of growers known by some as The Three Musketeers. They espoused the motto, "All for one and one for all," which was not a superficial concept in Jerome. It was very much part of the ethos of the hippie community, and of the community of former miners and others that were stranded in Jerome when the mines closed. You saw what needed to be done and you helped each other, heart-to-heart and shoulder-to-shoulder, focused on the tasks of the work to be done, and not on the differences between you.

The betrayal of that ethos from within the community by a long-time friend was a sad and unforgivable apostasy.

One of the more striking characteristics of Jerome was that the community transcended the individual. It did so in the mining days and it did so in the time of the bust.

Part of what was lost after that bust was the freedom we had to live outside of society's definition of a good and wholesome life. It was not just about pot. It was about the freedom to be who you were, accepted for your idiosyncrasies, and not be forced to hide.

That freedom lasted for at about a decade. It had played out within the context of our community and was the result of a lot of communal effort. It was one of the great pleasures of living here. It was rare to have the freedom to live out our peculiarities within a community that wholly accepted them.

The raid closed us emotionally. It burst our bubble of openhearted friendliness and trust. Were there other rats among us, we wondered. Those of us that smoked became furtive out of necessity. Those of us lucky enough to find decent pot were careful not to disclose the sources. Our stashes were carefully hidden and we pulled out only small portions at a time.

Newcomers to Jerome, whether they rented or bought homes here, no matter whose friend they were and what their bona fides, were given the polite chill for years after the raid. It was difficult for them to make friends. They could be narcs or snitches.

And that included my brother, who showed up in Paul and Jerry's Saloon one night dressed in shiny shoes, tie, and jacket. "Diane and Walter told me to come here to ask how to get to their house." The bartender and people in the bar said they did not know anyone named Diane and Walter. My brother bought a beer and persisted. Finally, the exasperated bartender asked, "Why do you want to know?" "Diane's my sister." "Oh," said a few people in chorus, "*That* Diane and Walter."

The Big Spliff

About a year after the pot bust of 1985, the Clarkdale Elementary School set up a precursor to the Drug Abuse Resistance Education (D.A.R.E.) program. Mr. Steele, the fifth-grade teacher, brought in a policeman, whom he introduced as Officer Friendly.

My son Max and his best friend Omar politely listened and watched the videos and movies about how smoking pot led directly to heroin, meth, crack, and cocaine addictions. Alcohol was seldom mentioned. They tried to figure out how the information presented squared with all the adults they knew that only smoked pot and seemed pretty mellow. Although their parents were not involved in the bust, Max and Omar knew about it and accepted their parents' position that few pot smokers were ever involved in violent crime.

After every educational program, Officer Friendly invited the kids to rat out their families or friends. "It'll be a secret between us," Officer Friendly said. Max and Omar had heard the stories about the snitch and the big bust in Jerome, they knew that a snitch was the worst kind of person.

At the end of the semester, the kids were asked to present skits about what they had learned. Max and Omar paired up and were the last to make a presentation.

They went into the hall to get into their costumes. When they walked back into the classroom, Omar had transformed himself into a cliché of the drug dealer—trench coat, big pockets, hat pulled over his forehead, sunglasses, and gold chains. Even though he was not yet twelve, he was almost six feet tall and his size made kids think he was formidable, and not to be messed with. However, Omar had a very tender heart and never got into fights.

Max had changed into a clean shirt, pressed trousers—the epitome of the kind of clean-cut kid who you would never associate with drugs. He was shorter than Omar by a foot and a half, fair-haired and fair-skinned. He had a beatific smile that made him look, well, maybe not quite angelic, but perhaps trustworthy—a kid every mom could be proud of. Max and Omar were best friends: Omar was the gentle giant and Max was the off-beat sidekick.

"Hey Max," says Omar. "I just got some dynamite Panama Red. Want to smoke a joint?"

"Oh no, Omar, but thanks anyway," Max said.

"How about some Maui Zowie that my friend just brought back from Hawaii. You hardly ever see that around any more, Max. It's awesome."

"Sorry, Omar, I have to say no to Maui Zowie today." Max smiled.

Officer Friendly beamed. It was just the way he had taught the kids to respond when someone offered to get them high.

"But Max, Max, here's something I know you won't turn down. I got hold of an old Thai stick, and man, is that some heavy-duty pot."

All of a sudden, from under his shirt, Max whipped out an eight-inch long, cigar-thick spliff, rolled in newspaper, which he pretended to light. "Well, Omar, the thing is, I have some of my own."

After no more than five shocked seconds, the room erupted in a roar as the kids rocked with laughter. The teacher could not be heard over the pandemonium for quite a few minutes and ordered Max and Omar to go to the principal's office.

The principal was friendly with many Jerome parents and was known in some circles for his own hell-raising ways.

"Look," he said to Max and Omar. "We know what goes on up there, but you don't have to parade it around. Try and mellow out."

Max and Omar became heroes. For years, the kids told the story to one another. After all, Max and Omar had "dared" the powers that be. And, maybe more importantly, they got away with it.

Faernstrom Becomes a Ghost

Faernstrom was arrested in Las Vegas, Nevada, in February 1987, and charged with the theft of a 1972 Ford pickup in Bullhead City.[79] He was jailed in Kingman, Arizona.

However, the charge of auto theft was dropped so that Faernstrom could be transferred to a jail in Prescott, Arizona, to stand trial on the original charge of cultivation of marijuana in Clear Creek. The prosecutors claimed that Faernstrom failed "to testify against suspects in the drug raid." Faernstrom's lawyer was adamant that Faernstrom had completed the terms of his agreement, namely to wear a wire. Apparently, there was nothing in the agreement that said he would testify to the legitimacy of the recordings. Faernstrom pled guilty to one count of possession of marijuana and was given three years probation with the proviso that he abstain from alcohol.

Faernstrom left Prescott that day and was not seen or heard from again until twenty-three years later, when he signed up to listen to Jerome's Gulch Radio's website. He posted a Facebook page that said he lived in Reno, Nevada.

Faernstrom died of cancer on January 2, 2013. The friend who took care of him while he was ill wrote me to ask, "What the hell did he ever do to y'all out in Jerome. Your blog just makes him sound like a dick without saying why! The James I knew was a loving, kind man who wouldn't hurt an enemy, and he is sorely missed." The reference to my blog was a series of articles I posted about the bust, which I pulled after I received a publishing deal.

I sent him the shortest factual version I could think of and quoted from articles about the raid in the *Arizona Republic.*

His friend wrote back: "I am stunned. His ashes sit beside the very computer I am writing on. He was my good friend. A mentor. A teacher with whom I will not break faith. Forgive my reaction, if you can. Of course, James never told me this side of the story. He spoke of Jerome with both love and longing, asking me, in his final days, to spread his ashes in Prescott National Forest—to take my Harley and grant him that one last ride. I can't imagine what led him to hurt everyone like that. Please know that he always spoke of his life there in the most glowing terms, so much so that my wife and I have given serious thought to relocating. He ended a good man."[80]

This letter is the only clue that those of us who knew Faernstrom have of what it meant for him to live imprisoned in himself and stay silent about his exile from the community he loved and the friends he betrayed.

Fourteen
Mercury Manufacturing Strikes it Rich

The growth of Jerome Instrument Corporation (JIC), a manufacturer of high quality mercury detectors, was an offset to Jerome's pot economy. After the busts, JIC's legitimacy and profitability helped provide a bridge to creating a viable tourist economy.

John McNerney, founder of the company, moved to Jerome in 1973. He made custom furniture, which he sold to doctors in Phoenix. He volunteered to help rework Jerome's planning and design policies and reorganize the fire department. His wife, Iris, became a server at the Candy Kitchen restaurant.

Eureka Moment

During summers, John had been hired to prospect for gold in the northern Nevada deserts. He came up with an idea to use accurate measurements of mercury vapor to find gold. "Mercury and gold ore often exist near one another," John said. "Mercury is easier to detect because it lets off gasses—volatilizes—in the soil. Under a hot desert sun, the soil heats up, causing the mercury vapor to rise upward. If I figure out how to accurately measure the amount of mercury vapor, I would have a window deep down into the earth that could lead to a deeply buried gold deposit." So far he wasn't having any luck translating his idea into a practical system.

John's chance encounter with an entomologist in a bar in Tuscarora supplied a possible solution. "He was counting bug populations by driving down the highway with a large tube stuck out of the window of his truck," John said. "At the end of the tube was an electrified screen. As bugs stuck to the screen, the electrical resistance of the screen increased and he was able to measure their concentrations. Who knows how he came up with this novel idea. I got to thinking about it when it occurred to me that the bugs were like the mercury gas atoms. Maybe their adsorption onto a gold-plated screen would cause an electrical interference that could be measured."

It was John's eureka moment.

With the help of some Arizona State University (ASU) professors, John put together some gold-plated screens and headed back out into the desert. He would use the screens to collect mercury vapor. As he headed into the desert on his motorbike, he had the ingenious idea for collecting higher concentrations of mercury vapor over the soil by hooking up the gold screens to a portable car vacuum cleaner.

"This seemed to be working quite well," John told me. "Then, out in the distance I notice two cowboys on horses. I figure they're looking for stray cattle. They notice me on my hands and knees and start coming closer. Maybe they think I need help. Maybe they're flashing on those Western movies where some bedraggled guy is dragging his ass across a sandy desert because he's out of water. They urge their horses closer.

"That's when they notice I have a vacuum cleaner in my hands and seem to be hosing the desert. The cowboys are dumbfounded. Nobody could think of anything to say. There is no common language for what is happening. The cowboys turn and ride away."

Humble Beginnings

John's idea for using gold film to attract mercury vapor became the basis for a superior detector. For the next four years, John was unable to sell his idea to anyone. Various analytical companies from as far away as New Jersey and Japan invited him to demonstrate his prototype. They would give John the royal treatment. Then the "not quite yet being manufactured syndrome" would set in. Silence. He would hear nothing further from them.

John received an order for a mercury detector from out of the blue in 1977 from one of ASU's graduating geology students. The order galvanized John to raise the start-up money for a manufacturing facility.

John spoke with Earl Bell, a laser scientist, at a 1978 New Year's Eve party in Paul and Jerry's Saloon. Earl was a genius inventor who never went to college, had honorary degrees from Stanford, and held many patents, including one on mercury gas ion lasers. He was the founder of Spectra-Physics, Inc., the first commercial laser company. When John told Earl that he wanted to build mercury detectors, but needed a place, Earl offered to rent him space for $50 a month in a building near the Verde Exploration mine. Bell had once used it as a small research lab.

Peter Buseck and John Holloway, two of John's favorite ASU professors, invested $10,000 each for start-up capital.

John called the instrument the Jerome Gold Film Mercury Analyzer and the business was off and running. Two years later he rented one of the large high school buildings from Verde Exploration and began a full-scale operation that soon had annual sales of five million dollars.

When friends and colleagues teased him about basing his company in a dilapidated town full of hippies, John said, "I never wanted to work in a concrete bunker."

John McNerney and his employees at Jerome Instrument Corporation in late 1980, just after the company moved from Earl Bell's old lab near the Douglas Mansion. Front step left: Nell Moffett. Second step L-R: Paul Nonnast, Esther Burton, Darrell Fellers. Third step L-R: Iris McNerney, John McNerney, Kathy Davidson. Fifth step L-R: Stephanie Ballatore, Karen Gorman, Mary Nickerson, Susan Kinsella, Barbara Blackburn. Sixth step L-R: Lindsey Waddell, Ed Dowling, Randy Murdock. Upper step: Sandra Strong, Carol Nesselrode, Pat Montreuil, Roger Davis. Courtesy John McNerney.

A Perfect Kodak Moment

Sales could be counted on the fingers of one hand during JIC's first year. Their second order came from Eastman Kodak, which needed to ensure that mercury vapor would not interfere with the silver nitrate used in their film processes.

John delivered the detector and set it up for a demonstration. Fifty employees hovered around the podium.

"I turned it on and the detector just blew up: smoke, sparks, small-scale fireworks. Incredible. I was so surprised that I just started laughing and so did everyone else. I called the guy who helped put together the wiring harness and we troubleshot the problem over the phone. I fixed it and demonstrated the prototype successfully the next day."

Togetherness on a Scale You Never Even Dreamed of

Between 1981 and 1983, John recruited fifty employees and many subcontractors from the four hundred people in Jerome. The need for paying jobs was enormous, particularly for many people that stayed on the sidelines of Jerome's pot industry, participated in town politics, and wanted a way to support themselves and their eccentric lifestyles.

John could recognize someone's skills in one field and assumed they could adapt them to another. "Maybe tourists only saw hippies, but in the four years I had lived here, I knew that many of my employees would be those so-called hippies. Many were geniuses. This tiny town was able to spit out all the talent I needed."

Barbara Blackburn was a former vice president of Wells Fargo Bank in San Francisco. She had the specialized skills to manage personnel and set up computer systems to track them. When John hired her, the only job she had been able to find was bartending for less than minimum wage. She became president of the company. "She was a cut-loose hippie on weekends; but an extremely sophisticated financial professional during the week. She helped us grow into a first-rate company."

John hired artist Paul Nonnast to design the detector's case based on a hamster cage that Paul had designed for a child's pet—an incredible labyrinth full of spinning balls and intricate ramps all done with phenomenal craftsmanship and imagination. "I didn't know much about Paul," John said, "but that cage made me want to. It was as though he had gotten inside the head of a hamster and designed from there."

I developed my promotional and writing skills in the music business when I worked as an artist's manager for Bill Graham's Fillmore Management. When I formed an advertising and public relations company in 1982, John snapped up my proposal to be our first client. I did everything from write operation manuals to brochure copy and articles that got published in technical magazines. My partner, artist Gary Romig, was known for his watercolors of birds. He designed JIC's logo, brochures, and ads.

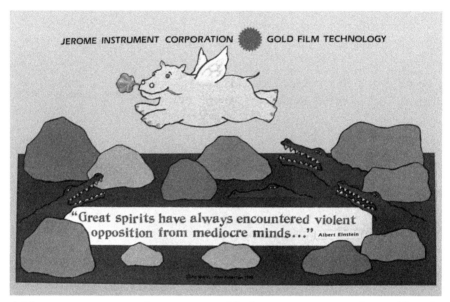

Ad for Jerome Instrument Corporation's Gold Film Mercury Detector designed by Ad Works' partners Diane Rapaport and Gary Romig. Illustration by Pam Fullerton.

Jamie Moffett, who helped build wiring harnesses and internal software, was a former computer engineer. John found that jewelers were very good at assembly work. "Engineers who visited JIC and looked inside the instrument were always amazed at the meticulousness of the work," John said. "Many commented it looked like a piece of art."

However, an all-Jerome crew did have an unexpected downside. "I soon found that I was hiring not just their skills but their idiosyncrasies, many of which I couldn't even have imagined existed. Nothing was secret; everyone hung out their eccentricities like so much laundry on a line. After work I'd meet my employees and their friends in one of the town's two bars. A few hours later, I'd be at a meeting to figure out how to raise money for fire safety equipment. The parties at Ferne Goldman's were particularly outrageous and drew everyone from JIC, a lot of the pot growers, many jewelers and artists—smokers, acid takers, and alcoholics. To live and work in Jerome was to experience togetherness on a scale you've never even dreamed of."

Paul Nonnast's Incredible Hamster Cage

"Ah, that hamster cage," said Amy Waddell. "You don't know how many times I've told the story of this tall man—whose intensity scared me a little as a kid—eyes fixed on whatever he was working on, always sweating a little from that innate focus. I remember tiptoeing up the steep narrow splintered steps to his apprentice studio and pushing open the trap door to see all of his colorful spheres floating above me. He created magic worlds, Paul!

"Perhaps it was his idea to make it, perhaps mine, and perhaps I knew nothing about it until the moment I walked upstairs to his room one day and he unveiled it. I was very young, maybe seven or eight years old. The circular cage was a thing of beauty—about two feet in height and two and a half feet in diameter. A thin mesh ran all the way around the circular top and bottom plywood plates. There was a pole up the middle of the cage, and tiny pegs created a circular staircase from top to bottom with little kidney bean-shaped platforms that extended out at various levels. Then there was a large gourd strung up about an inch from the bottom, acting as a little womblike swing. I believe Paul made a rather large habit-trail in there, as well. A fine ramp started at floor level then wound up all the way around the cage.

"I was beyond thrilled. It was so beautiful. I couldn't wait to put my hamster inside.

"The hamster was in Nonnast heaven. It ran the habit-trail, drank from the large bottle affixed to the side of the cage, ventured up the ramp. I remember his little black eyes and little pink ears and his little fuzzy body as he traipsed around his magnificent new digs—from pauper to royalty for no apparent reason."[81]

Mad as a Hatter

People that worked for JIC knew that mercury vapor was toxic to the nervous system and could make people "mad as a hatter," a term used to describe the shaking fits that hat makers got from working with mercury-laden felt.

The toxicity of mercury vapor led to markets John never dreamed of when he designed the instrument. He thought geologists would buy the instrument as a gold prospecting tool. His brother thought that dentists would buy them to measure the toxicity in offices that used mercury for dental fillings. A percentage of dentists committed suicide every year, apparently because mercury made them a little crazy.

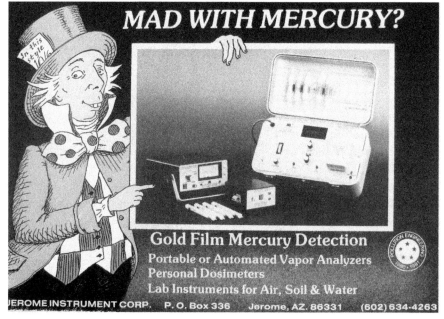

Ad for Jerome Instrument Corporation's Gold Film Mercury Detector designed by Ad Works' partners Diane Rapaport and Gary Romig. Illustration by Pam Fullerton.

Although some sales did go to these markets, the largest sales went to the U.S. Navy for use in its fleet of submarines and to hospitals for use in baby incubators. Vapor from broken mercury-based instrumentation is very toxic to people that depend on recirculated air in closed environments.

The Boss with a Social Conscience

John McNerney put profits for company stockholders at the bottom of his list. "Making an excellent product was number one. We strived for an aesthetic product with zero defects. I tried to follow a motto I had once seen on the lintel of a Colonial period industrial structure, 'Industry without beauty is drudgery.'

"We priced the detector at five times that of our competition," John said. "Our technology was superior and so was our instrument."

Treating employees well was John's second priority. From the begin-

152

ning, JIC instituted a liberal profit-sharing plan for employees. "The only people that were exempt were myself, Iris, two members of the management team, and the sales force which worked on liberal commissions. The board of directors set a profit objective for the year—anything greater than that margin went straight into the profit-sharing pool. This running total was updated monthly and presented in an image that resembled the old United Way goal fundraising thermometer. The financial statements were open to any employee and everyone always knew exactly where we stood. Seniority or job description was irrelevant. The staff from production, R&D, and administration shared equally in the profits. The plan guaranteed incentives for employees that cross-trained and filled in where needed. Quality never suffered, and no one, me included, worked more than forty hours a week. The employees resolved all employee problems. We were almost self-managing."

John McNerney holding one of his instruments, with the town of Jerome in the background. Photo by ML Lincoln.

Stockholder considerations were last. "If we could satisfy our customers with an excellent product, produce it with employees that were having a good time and were proud of their work, the stockholders would be well rewarded. And they were."

John McNerney encouraged civic volunteerism. "The company is one of the few in this area that doesn't penalize employees for participating on

153

company time," said Doug Dowis, the company's marketing manager and a Jerome volunteer fireman. "When there's a fire, we're told to drop whatever we're doing and go put it out. When there are training sessions in Phoenix, we're encouraged to attend. We're paid for doing it." Many JIC employees volunteered in projects ranging from coaching sports teams to working on school boards to becoming members of planning and zoning boards.

The company hired teenagers under a work-study scholarship program. The company matched the teenager's savings up to seventy-five dollars per month. When he went to college, Tony Rocha had accumulated $3,157 in his fund. "When I was sixteen my friends had jobs filling grocery bags and flipping hamburgers," Tony said. "Working in a high tech environment was totally different. What stands out in my memory was that the company listened to what I had to say. I got a real great feeling when they valued my opinion as much as that of a forty year old who had been working there ten years. When I left to go to college, I knew I could go out and get a job anywhere."

"Giving to the community has no monetary value," John McNerney said. "Providing scholarships doesn't add to the bottom line. But when you encourage civic activity or education you help upgrade and enrich the quality of the community life and that helps make life more rewarding and work more meaningful. If we set an admirable standard, maybe others will follow."

John sold JIC to Arizona Instrument Corporation (AZIC) in 1988. Many of JIC's subcontractors, including myself, were hired by the new company, which made for an easy transition when the company left town.[82]

New Adventures

John and Iris sold their home for a good profit and moved away. They were still relatively young and ready for new adventures. The money they realized from the sale of the business and home left them with enough money to fund the rest of their life without needing to start a new business.

Their first adventure was to move to Port Townsend, Washington, where John built a most beautiful boat that took them on many voyages. A favorite was sailing the islands that were near La Paz, Baja California.

Eventually they moved to Todos Santos, in Baja California, where John built a home and most of the furniture for it.

He became an environmental activist. He serves on the board of directors of an environmental organization called *Niparaja*, which is devoted to marine conservation and the protection of many of the sensitive environmental coastal areas and islands that he grew to love while sailing.

He is most proud of helping to spearhead a grass roots movement to protest the opening of a Canadian-owned open pit gold mine. It was to be located near the watershed of the Sierra Laguna, very close to a dam that provides most of the water for Todos Santos and other cities and villages. The movement had the rallying cry of *"Aqua Vale mas que Oro"* (Water has more Value than Gold). The protest movement was successful in preventing the opening of the mine.

"You could say that my life has come full circle," John said. "I used to be involved in helping mining companies find new sources of gold. The world needs metals, but mined responsibly. No one needs any more gold."

Fifteen
Renaissance of the Arts

The first newcomer to rent property from the Jerome Historical Society was the celebrated American artist, Roger Holt, who had exhibited at the Metropolitan Museum of Art, Corcoran Gallery, and Carnegie Institute. Holt and his wife, Shan, arrived in 1954 and they lived in Jerome until the mid-1960s.

Holt rented a gallery and studio in the Starr building (now Arizona Discoveries). "Due to rains, it was wetter inside than out," said Holt, referring to the day he moved in. The Jerome Historical Society voted $295 to help make repairs.

Holt was known as an eccentric. He and Shan were regulars at the bars. Billy Watt, whose father bought the Spirit Room in 1963, remembered that Shan and Roger would wrap their heads in toilet paper turbans and lead patrons in snake dances down Main Street. "When he came back, Roger would down another whiskey and tell us he was heading off to knock out another painting."

Billy's mother, Faye, collected some of Holt's paintings, as did Tom and Frankie (Francis) Vincent, who owned the Ford dealership in Cottonwood. They moved to Jerome in the 1960s.

Shan founded a group called the Verde Valley Artists. The historical society

Roger Holt was a nationally recognized painter who moved to Jerome in 1954. His wife, Shan Holt, started the Verde Valley Artists association. Photo by Art Clark from Ballad of Laughing Mountain. *Courtesy Jerome Historical Society (2003-076-028).*

donated space in the New State Motor Company building. A wall separated the artists from the U.S Post Office. Shan found a patron and friend in portrait artist, Lilli Brant, who became president of the group. As the town struggled to survive, Lilli's husband, geophysicist Arthur Brant, predicted that someday Jerome would become an art destination.

"Jerome with its romantic past and its aerie perch ... could well become a tourist MUST and an art Mecca; for seldom is it possible to find so combined the artistic appeal of the tortuous, hilly streets, and slumping, but individualistic and animative houses with the breathtaking panorama swept out in varying pastel shades for miles at one's very feet."[83]

His words were prophetic.

The Verde Valley Art Association

The Verde Valley Artists became the Verde Valley Art Association (VVAA) in 1975 and it was still housed in the New State Motor Company building. It flourished in ways that were only hoped for in previous decades.

More than one hundred newcomers called themselves painters, sculptors, jewelers, carvers, potters, writers, and musicians. Many joined the VVAA and helped put on group shows.

One of VVAA's earliest efforts was to assemble a show for the Arizona State Capitol Rotunda, as part of the United States bicentennial celebration.

The exhibit featured seventy-nine pieces of work from thirty-two Jerome artisans. The pieces were exotic, whimsical, and diverse: a gourd-stitch pouch by David Santillan (the only exhibitor who had been born in Jerome); Mimi Currier's sculpture, "Jerome Water," which was a mule with water panniers laying under a black coral twig. It was made of pipestone, black coral, jet, ebony, sericite, and silver. Nancy Driver's sheepskin teddy bear; sculptor Scott Owens' serpentine piece, "Cowpie and Mushrooms"; a carved eagle from Craig Bacharach that was inlaid by Lee Louden with ivory, jet, and oyster shell; a feathered necklace from Diane Koble; vests from Ferne Goldman with their secret pot pockets; a delicate black walnut rocker by John McNerney, who remembers Ferne—all three hundred pounds of her—plopping into the rocker. She barely fit inside its arms and he wondered whether she would crash it (she did not).

The VVAA hired a director in 1977. Board president, Mimi Currier, wrote the ad, which included: "Macramé artists looking to achieve stardom need not apply." The group hired Hank Chaikin, a longhaired hippie who had produced art shows and started a foreign film club for Yavapai College.

He remembers his first meeting with Mimi, whom he described as a powerful woman. "What do you want me to do?" Hank asked. "You can do whatever you want and if we don't like it, we'll let you know," Mimi said. His job was to balance the nonprofit goal of the VVAA, which was to bring in outside shows *and* provide a commercial art gallery for local artists.

The grants that Chaikin secured enabled the VVAA to employ four full-time people. He made the VVAA a certified workplace for young people enrolled in the the Comprehensive Employment and Training Act (CETA) program.

He began a student art show that toured the state and garnered support from many Verde Valley businesses, which had been standoffish and suspicious of Jerome.

Most importantly, he started featuring non-Jerome artists for major Jerome exhibitions. One featured Paolo Soleri, the Italian architect who built the futuristic desert city Arcosanti, which was based on the fusion of architecture and ecology. Soleri called this fusion arcology. Another show featured Lew Davis, dean of Arizona artists, who grew up in Jerome during its mining days. Musician Pat Jacobsen and jeweler Susan Dowling went to Phoenix in Pat's pickup truck and borrowed all of Davis' paintings from museums and collectors, including the Herbergers (Kay Herberger was the grand patroness of the arts in Arizona; her $12 million gift to ASU ensured

The Major Lingo band started in the early 1980s and remained popular in Arizona until they gave their last concert on New Year's Eve 2013. Photo by Richard Kimbrough, courtesy John Ziegler.

that art, dance, music, and theater programs would flourish). "It was a fabulous show," said Susan.

The VVAA shows of Arizona artists helped place Jerome on the map as an art destination.

Within Jerome, the VVAA gave artists a focal point to meet and exchange ideas. Shows introduced their art, and for many gave them their first sales.

From these beginnings, Jerome would become the major art mecca that many had dreamed about and worked hard to achieve.

The VVAA morphed into The Jerome Artists Cooperative Gallery and moved into the lobby of the Hotel Jerome in 1990.

Art, Business, and Politics

One of Jerome's unusual qualities was that art, business, and politics were not separate entities.

In a town that had a hundred volunteer positions, artists quickly learned that if they wanted a say in how the town was rescued, they needed to participate. Artists helped draft Jerome's Comprehensive Plan and Zoning and Design Review ordinances. Potter Dave Hall was chief of the fire department in the 1980s and many artists, men and women, were volunteer firefighters and members of the auxiliary. John McNerney, founder of Jerome Instrument Corporation and furniture maker, was a member of the fire department. Ceramicist and painter Jane Moore and artist Anne Bassett, furniture maker Richard Martin, and luthier Lew Currier served on the Town Council for many years. Writer and singer Katie Lee served on the board of the Jerome Historical Society. Carver Mimi Currier ran as a candidate for the Arizona State Senate. Her platform included a plea for legislators to support the arts and arts organizations. "Arizona needs to make a strong link between tourism and art," she said. Thirty-five Arizona artists, many of them from Jerome, donated work to be publicly auctioned to support her candidacy.

A number of artists founded their own businesses.

In the 1970s: Dave Hall's Made in Jerome Pottery; Emiliano's, an artist cooperative; Ferne Goldman's Downhill Trading Company; Jim Rome's gallery; Ashley Hofstetter's gallery; Nancy Driver's Wounded Buffalo Leathers; Lew Currier's luthier shop; and Richard Martin's furniture shop, Woodchute Woodworks.

Jeweler Curt Pfeffer and jewelry designer and ceramicist Sharon Watson built a new building on Main Street in 1984 and opened Aurum Jewelry, which displayed the work of Verde Valley jewelers and artists. Photographer and filmmaker ML Lincoln opened The Exposure Gallery in the Hotel Jerome before it became the Jerome Artists Cooperative and put on shows by Jerome artists Diane Geoghegan and Paul Nonnast. Painters and sculptors Robin Anderson and Margo Mandette drew hundreds of visitors every month to their beautiful gallery in the high school.

Dave Hall built a new building at the end of Main Street in the 1990s for Made in Jerome Pottery. Potter Tracy Weisel built the Raku Gallery near Spook Hall and renovated the ruins of La Victoria Market into a glass blowing studio. Many other artists opened galleries either uptown or in the old high school complex.

Some artists helped to brand Jerome businesses. Painter Gary Romig designed the logos for the Verde Valley Art Association and illustrator Pam Fullerton drew a flying hippo being pursued by alligators to illustrate a quote by Albert Einstein: "Great spirits have always encountered violent opposition from mediocre minds" for a poster for JIC. Architect and sculptor Paul Nonnast designed the logo for Richard Flagg's rafting tours, Sacred Monkey Expeditions. Photographer Michael Thompson took color photographs for musician/vintner James Maynard Keenan's Caduceus Cellars and took publicity photos for Jerome musicians and artists. Singer and web master Noel Fray designed websites for several Jerome businesses.

Many artists named above came here in the seventies and, with few exceptions, still live in Jerome.

I wanted to spotlight a few of these artists to give readers a flavor of the quirky eccentricity mixed with excellence so many embody. So as not to offend anyone with my choices (we all have favorites), I chose three close friends, Katie Lee, and Wylci Fables and Jore Park.

The Art of Synchronous Energy

Wylci Fables and Jore Park came to Jerome in 1980 and rented the old music room that was on the second floor above the gym in the old high school complex—a 40x50-foot room with blond maple floors and large windows with unimpeded views of the Verde Valley. The space looked like something between a circus set, an art studio, and a camping experiment—trapeze bars on the ceiling, big tent in the corner, cook stove, a jumble of musical instruments, paints, dyes, shoji screens, rice paper rolls, and television screens.

Among the many eccentric people that were drawn to Jerome, Wylci and Jore stood out, never to be missed in any crowd. Jore looked like a Gauguin primitive—big and stocky, large boned, with a surprising feline grace. Wylci, whose name was based on a pun, "we'll see," was delicately boned, nimble, and ethereal looking.

They were the first white people I met that braided their hair in corn-rows, each woven with a different colored ribbon. They wore clothes of harlequin colors—turquoise, magenta, orange, black, purple. Those colors dominated their paintings, too. Their toenails and fingernails were painted in hues of black and purple.

They would float down the street, and sometimes whirl around each other, exuberantly jubilant. Tourists stared and wondered, *"Who are they?"*

Jore said she first started drawing with Wylci and came to understand emotionally what he meant when he painted green and then put yellow next to it. "Then I'd take a brush and draw some lines with a little blue." They found a common language, a synchronous method to work together that made it quite impossible to tell who did what. They did everything as a team, without a shred of separateness or contention, a continuous dance. They were seldom apart. I cannot remember a time when I was alone with either of them.

They created mixed media art that was wildly experimental even when judged by avant-garde standards and they pushed beyond boundaries that no one had ever considered.

The first Wylci and Jore art I saw was a short video that contained the screech of a strange jungle bird intertwined with colorful translucent abstract paintings; shapes that morphed into the movement of oily liquid colors; and the grey shadows of Wylci and Jore as they danced and passed through each other. The sounds and movements increased in a maddening intensity, and suddenly ended.

The wildest project for a new video "Ouije" began with them creating a 1-foot by 60-foot abstract painting, using wax and dyes on rice paper. It looked like a choreographed dance.

They gathered a ragtag orchestra of twelve musicians from Jerome's rock and country bands, the Phoenix symphony, a jazz saxophonist from Sedona, and a percussionist who wore leopard shorts and brought in an exotic collection of African drums, sticks, gongs, bells, and cymbals.

The painting became a musical score that was videotaped and shown at a rate of one foot per second on a large television. Wylci and Jore each conducted half the musicians with such instructions as, "This is where the

Flier for Wylci and Jore's recording event in Jerome in 1982. Drawing by Wylci Fables and Jore Park. Original from Diane Rapaport collection.

cheetah meets the ping pong player and it all shifts to blue." The musicians would play their interpretation of these strange directives.

Everyone worked very seriously for three days, while my husband Walter recorded it and I stood around and marveled at the sheer incongruity of it all. The result was an abstract three-minute cacophony that for all its strangeness held together with unmistakable artistic clarity. The music became part of the video.

Then Wylci and Jore decided to make money so they could go to Japan. They painted extraterrestrial-like translucent shapes on rice paper with wax and dyes, a choreographed dance of colors that ribboned in and out of each other. It was their most accessible work and a number of Jeromans bought some of the paintings and helped send them to Tokyo.

While there, they made a video, "Relax Before You Swim," which featured their friend Robin in underwater gear walking through the Toyko subway and then riding on a train. She was "smoking a cigarette, at one point blowing the smoke right out of her snorkel pipe, looking over the shoulders of the commuters reading newspapers on the train, trying to talk to them in the station in Japanese, and generally outraging many of the Japanese who promptly pretended not to see her," said Wylci. "The rest of the video depicted the moods of the commuters (exhausted, isolated, or alternatively giggling) and street scenes including us walking through the dense crowd in the train station with a paper puppet sticking way above the heads of the Japanese," said Jore. It was a brilliant, funny, and disturbing work.

A few years after their trip to Japan, Wylci and Jore moved to Maui, built a cottage and a home, and raised two sons.

When I visited them in 2012, they were working on multiple projects: a novel called *Slow Truth*, set in a fictional version of Jerome; the construction of images using their proprietary software that deconstructs and reconstructs images using light and pattern analysis to shape the viewer's sensory and emotional response built using a visual language developed from the original wax and dye imagery created in Jerome; the creation of ninety-second video news collages with broad themes such as women, art, and music, each short work visual tagged to its source, whether it was speeches, music, or videos. The videos reveal their first glimmers of teaching their software to assemble video imagery (http:///syngenie.com); and on perfecting a text to video global visual language and messaging system (http://vizlingo.com). Their energy to create is as boundless, innovative, and exuberant as it was in Jerome.

I asked them to describe Jerome's special magic. "It was always the people that made Jerome so magical, embodiments of the mountain spirits that haunt the place," they said. "The spectrum of characters that would show up for a performance on a moments notice was inspiring. One would expect a city like San Francisco to be able to produce an audience of a hundred for a cutting-edge performance, but for Jerome with its population of what, four hundred at the time, to be able to do so was just an amazing show of support. I'd have to check the gravitational anomaly maps made by the GOCE satellite, but I would not be surprised to see Jerome show up with a super dense direct connection to the earth's core, something the ancient tribes and the modern day sensitives knew already!" (GOCE—Gravity Field and Steady-State Ocean Circulation Explorer)

Do Any Famous Artists Live in Jerome?

I was once asked, "Do any famous artists live in Jerome?" I thought about this and answered, "Katie Lee."

She is famous in Jerome for riding her bike through town naked except for a helmet and boots when she was seventy-seven years old. She howled with laughter as she sailed the mile downhill from Main Street to her house. It was her way to shed the glum, sad feelings she had after a close Jerome friend died.

Side view of the ceramic bowl that Jane Moore made for Katie Lee's 93rd birthday. Photo by Katie Lee.

Katie on her bike. Ceramicist and painter Jane Moore's birthday present to singer songwriter and anti-dam activist Katie Lee was a ceramic bowl commemorating Katie's famous stark-naked bike ride through Jerome. Photo by Katie Lee.

The day she decided to do it was the kind of sticky and hot day it gets just before a summer monsoon. "Friends were snapping at each other like loony birds in a tank of toxins and the humidity was a wet, down comforter under a 110-degree heating pad."[84]

She rode past bar owner Paul Vojnic as he talked with Ray, the town cop. Paul said, "Well, aren't you going to arrest her?" "What am I going to arrest her for," Ray said, "for floppy tits?"

Even before Katie reached her house, people who saw her started the phone calls shaking with their laughter. "Do you know what Katie Lee just did?"

Katie says she's likely to be more famous for her *ride* than for her books and music.

***

She'll always be famous in my mind for introducing me to the open, unbridled wilderness West. I had never before spent a night that was not in a national park, with groomed trails, signs that told you where to go, what time to set up for the right light to catch a photograph, and sanitary campgrounds you had to reserve. I had never backpacked nor rafted a white-water river.

Katie took me to pristine wildernesses without trails or cairns where we were unlikely to meet another person. Armed with topo maps, she would march off down some canyon and mark the route with a highlighter pen. She had two rules: don't go down something you can't get up by yourself, and don't tell anyone where you went.

On one ten-day backpacking trip in Utah near the sandstone canyons that she loved most of all, we went down one that hadn't been visited since Native Americans left in the fourteenth century. We found untrammeled ruins, whole pots, areas strewn with corncobs, grinding stones, and other remnants of a life long gone.

Katie is her most natural self—funny, easy to be around, helpful, uncritical—in these wild places. She is a gifted storyteller and those wonderful canyon amphitheaters inspired her and turned me into a rapt audience. The most magical moments were when she played her beat-up guitar and sang, and the coyotes added their wild harmonies.

I grew to appreciate why these lonesome places are shelters for our emotional upheavals and havens for spiritual growth.

At the end of one trip, which included a rappel down a steep canyon wall, we found a gravesite that had been plundered and we reported it. "How did you find it?" asked the ranger. Katie told him about the canyon that we had just come down. "We thought there wasn't a route through there," the ranger said. Within two years, the route was written about in a popular adventure magazine.

***

Katie was absolutely unforgettable to my mother after I introduced them at a party at Wylci and Jore's art studio.

My mom and Katie were contemporaries. Both were stunning women throughout their lives. Katie was a sensuous and provocative blue-eyed Irishwoman. My mother, a black-eyed beauty with a quick smile and a great deal of charm, was crowned Miss Greek America when she was eighteen. They were the center of attention in any room they entered.

165

Katie Lee in 2012 at the age of 93. Courtesy James 'Q' Martin.

Mom grew up in upper middle class Washington, D.C. surrounded by lawyers, bankers, and foreign embassy personnel. She and her husband lived with my paternal grandfather in Scranton, Pennsylvania, during the Depression and she watched the candy-making business that made him millions go downhill and reduce the family to poverty. The Scranton home was sold in 1940, and our family moved to Washington, D.C. My mother was the only one in our family to get a job. She was the first woman lawyer to be hired by the National Labor Relations Board. When Katie met her, Mom had just been appointed as an Administrative Law Judge for the same board.

Katie grew up like a Western fox, shrewd at survival and defense against predators. The downturn in real estate was her family's downfall in the Depression. She was western and country, a native Arizonan who grew up near the foothills of Tucson. She shot quail, squirrels, and rabbits for the stew pot with her .22 rifle. She camped in the mountains and canyons around Tucson with a couple of cowboys that taught her their songs and took her to the cantinas and brothels of Nogales, Mexico, where she learned Mexican border songs.

They met during my mom's second visit to Jerome. My mother could not believe that we had settled into this dilapidated town full of pot smokers. She thought smoking pot led directly to heroin and she lectured us about it every time she could. This second visit though, she made a little peace with Jerome. She said it reminded her of the mountainous northern Greek village that her parents had come from.

But nothing prepared her for the party at Wylci and Jore's. I told my mom she would meet my close friend Katie, whom I described as a well-known published author and singer/songwriter who was about her age. My mother smiled with relief at the possibility of meeting a *respectable* friend of mine.

Mom walked up the forty-five iron steps to the second floor of the gym. As soon as we were at the top, I handed her the brown paper bag that contained her high heels, which she primly substituted for her walking shoes. As we walked down the corridor, we could hear ripples of music and laughter. Soon we were immersed among fifty rowdy-looking hippies, gussied up in their gypsy best, a wilder and more raucous group than my mother had ever been in. I looked around for Katie so I could introduce them. But, it was not until I looked up that I found her as she swung upside down on a trapeze. The skirt that hung over her body exposed the white ruffled pantaloons she had sewn for the occasion. She waved her high heels, which were, oddly enough, the same color as Mom's.

It was an irresistible moment for me. I marched my mother up to Katie and introduced them. It was one of the few times I ever saw my mother at a total loss of words. Katie invited her to lunch the next day without missing a swing. Eventually, they became good friends that admired each other for their independent and outspoken natures.

***

Katie had an eclectic and wild-riding career. She began her professional career in 1948 as a stage and screen actress. She performed bit parts in motion pictures in Hollywood; had running parts on major NBC radio shows, including *The Great Gildersleeve* and *The Railroad Hour* with Gordon McRae; was a pioneer actress and folk music director on *The Telephone Hour* with Helen Parrish in the early '50s; then left Hollywood to spend ten years as a folk singer in coffeehouses and cabarets throughout the U.S., Canada, and Mexico. She was gifted at most everything she set out to do.

When I met her, she was the foremost documentarian of cowboys and their songs in western ranching circles. She brings them to life in her book *Ten Thousand Goddam Cattle: A History of the American Cowboy in Song, Story and Verse*; and in her recording *Ten Thousand Goddam Cattle*. The book might have been a bestseller among ranchers were it not for the *goddam* in the title. Ranchers are a conservative and religious lot. "It's the title of a famous song," she proclaimed and would hear of no entreaties to change it.

During the 1980s and 1990s, Katie performed at cowboy poetry gatherings in Ruidoso, New Mexico; Medora, North Dakota; and Elko, Nevada, among others. Those festivals revived the West's great legacy of cowboy songs, which are different from the songs sung at Country Western music festivals, which Katie loathes. "Country and Western is neither," she once told me in an interview for an article I wrote for *Sing Out!* (a folk song magazine). "Its lyrics are about tight miserable places like phone booths, dingy bars, and stuffy bedrooms and some poor twit whose wife or girlfriend just dumped him." She dismissed country superstar Waylon "f*#!ing" Jennings, "He wouldn't know a cowboy from a cow."

There's no mistaking what Katie felt about anything. "Tact is a f*#!ing waste of time," she once told me.

Katie is venerated as the most flamboyant of knights among a growing legion of pro-wilderness activists. She uses her pen, her voice, and her guitar to champion the draining of Powell Reservoir to restore the magical Glen Canyon that was drowned by it and to release the flow of the Colorado River within it. She refers to the reservoir as "Loch Latrine" and "Rez Foul." "Dam dams" reads her auto license plate.

Katie Lee loved to decorate her fence with political statements. This one was to "support" Hillary Clinton during the 2008 Democratic presidential primaries. Photo by Katie Lee.

"Why Glen Canyon," I asked her over lunch one day, even though I had read her book, *Glen Canyon Betrayed* and heard her recordings "Folk Songs of the Colorado River" and "Colorado River Songs." I was hoping my question would take her by surprise and that she might give me an answer that was not in her books. Without even a pause, she said, "Because Glen Canyon is always present in my mind, it's hardly ever in my dreams. It's as if my feet are still stuck in the sand at the edge of the river. It's where I live. This other life I walk around in all day—well, that's a passing thing. And in many ways it's my defense against the sadder mechanisms of life around us. And God knows we all need those mechanisms from keeping ourselves from going crazy in this mad world."

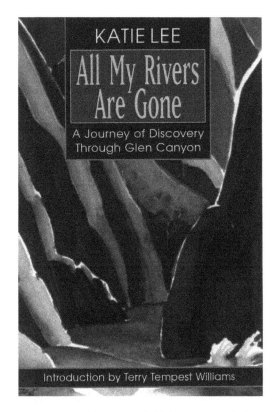

One of Katie Lee's books and one of her CD's, both paeans to Glen Canyon, a paradise lost under Reservoir Powell, which Katie calls Res Foul and sometimes Loch Latrine.

Dream Garden Press will publish Katie's latest book, *The Ghosts of Dandy Crossing*, in 2014. It is a historical novel about Katie's love affair with a handsome cowboy/river runner at the time when the Glen Canyon dam was being constructed and their lives were about to change irrevocably.

Kate Wolf Meets Katie Lee: Fires Burning Bright in Old Jerome

Singer songwriter Kate Wolf visited Jerome in 1983. Kate was among the first songwriters in the San Francisco Bay area to record and release recordings independent of major record companies.

Kate gave a concert in the Episcopal Church, which is used today as offices and archives for the Jerome Historical Society. The church was renovated in the early 1980s. It had a 250-seat performance center with a stage, rich maroon velvet curtains and red oak wood floors. An antique Bosendorfer grand piano that had been donated to the society added elegance and sophistication. The acoustics of the room were perfect; no sound system was needed for the concerts, plays, and lectures that filled the center.

The church for Kate's concert was packed. She filled the room with her haunting, melancholy voice.

After the concert, I introduced her to Katie Lee. She was sixty-four years old, dressed in peacock colors, charismatic and feisty. She was sharply blunt. "Kate, you're a hell of a performer, but I couldn't understand all your lyrics. Sometimes you mumble. You need to learn to enunciate. Lyrics are the most important thing; if nobody can understand you, you are singing to fresh air. Come by my house tomorrow and I'll help you as I was helped by some of the top professionals in the industry." They became instant friends.

Both loved wild flowing rivers and understood the importance of finding a sense of rootedness in wilderness places.

Katie arranged for Kate to stay at the house of a friend. A few days later, Kate played her newest song, "Old Jerome," at Katie's house. The song captured a town as it awakened to its new identity and the almost supernatural hold that it had on almost everyone that lived there.

(For Katie Lee) Words and music by Kate Wolf. Copyright 1983 by Another Sundown Publishing Company. Reprinted with permission.

Drinking early morning coffee, talking with good friends
and walking the streets of rough cut stone,
She was once a miners' city, then the ghost of a dying town,
now there's a fire burning bright in old Jerome.

Some have come for fortune, some have come for love
some have come for the things they cannot see

But the grass is green and growing where the gardens once had died
and the birds sing in the wild Ailanthus trees.

The sun comes up on Cleopatra
Where the mines lie sleeping far below
The wind and the rain sing an old mountain refrain
And the copper shines like Arizona gold

They say that once you live here, you never really leave
she'll have a hold on you until the day you die
With her ground moving crazy and her fierce wind blowing free
and her ruins standing proud against the sky

Old houses cling to mountains like miners cling to dreams
they hold on just so long and then let go
For the mountain is your mistress, you'll ride her 'til you fall
and wash down to the valley far below

The sun drops behind old Cleopatra
Where the mines lie sleeping far below
The wind and the rain sing a miner's old refrain
And the copper shines like Arizona gold

With their silent empty rooms that hold the old town's memories
and their doorways that reach out like empty arms

In the streets the children play, climbing up the crooked stairs,
and lovers touch and make their way back home
The sound of hammers echo in the once forgotten halls
and hope stirs in the heart of old Jerome

The moon shines down on Cleopatra
Where the mines lie sleeping far below
The wind and the rain sing an old ghost town refrain
And the copper shines like Arizona gold

Katie loved the song so much that she etched the fresh concrete outside her writing studio with one of its verses and sent Kate a photo of it. She persuaded the town of Jerome to adopt the entire song as its official anthem in 1987, and she performed "Old Jerome" on the TV special "Portraits of America."[85]

The Furor over the Hotel Jerome

Since art had played such a major role to lift Jerome out the doldrums, it was a great surprise when newly elected Mayor Francesca Segretti and the Jerome Town Council of 1990 voted to partition the historic Hotel Jerome into three shops. They spurned rental offers from several artists. The council voted $1,000 for remodeling work.

The mayor expressed interest in renting the choice window spot for an antique shop for herself; another council member wanted to display his art glass in the mayor's new shop. It was the first time since the mines closed that members of the Jerome Town Council blatantly used their political positions to further their own interests.

Eighty irate citizens swarmed into the next town meeting. They were armed with a long demand letter that set forth grievances and threatened a stop work injunction.[86]

The letter declared that it was the first time that a Town Council ever went against the goal of preserving the historical integrity of one of the most visible Main Street buildings. It had ignored a recommendation from Planning and Zoning and a proposal from artists to turn the entire floor into an artists' cooperative. And in so doing, the letter continued, the council ignored the goal of the town's Comprehensive Plan to "provide the facilities and maintain an atmosphere necessary to encourage artists to work and live in Jerome."

The letter strongly objected to the council's vote on the proposal that was posted as only a discussion meeting and demanded that the two council members interested in the space recuse themselves because of a conflict of interest and not participate in any further decision-making processes about the hotel.

The meeting was rancorous and emotional. The mayor stated that artists had no monetary value to the town and that the partitioned spaces would bring in far more to the town in sales tax revenues. The insult drew a huge uproar in the chambers, which caused her to stomp out in rage. Jane Moore called me in tears after the meeting and said she was going to resign her position as Chair of Planning and Zoning and would I put my name in for the position. "The artists have done so much for this town," she said. "We were instrumental in the town pulling itself together. I am so upset."

I was elected as chair and made a list of 125 or so artists that resided in Jerome, the dozens that owned businesses and the fifty or so that owned homes. I listed the names of the artists that had served on the more than a hundred volunteer positions such as the historical society, fire department, public library, and humane society. The council retracted its vote. Work on the lobby was stopped and the space became the Jerome Artists Cooperative Gallery that exists to this day.

Merger of Art and History

The Jerome Historical Society sponsored an art show in 1999 called "Images of Jerome: A Centennial Retrospective: 1899–1999." It depicted the culture of the community during three distinct periods: mining era, ghost town years, and restoration. A collection of more than one hundred paintings, photographs, jewelry, stained glass, tiles, sculpture, and pottery were displayed that were created by artists and artisans that lived in Jerome.

The show was an outpouring of Jerome's heart. The town was a jewel on the side of the mountain; an oasis with hundreds of varieties of trees.

I produced that show on behalf of the society. It was a propitious time to remind those of us who helped rescue the town of our deep attachments here and our roots into every aspect of its culture. Visitors recognized how deeply entwined art was in the collective identity of Jerome.

The art was gathered from about 150 homes, studios, and businesses in Jerome and from the society's collection in the Mine Museum. Curators ML Lincoln and Karen Mackenzie put in more than four hundred volunteer hours. They were astonished to find homes so chock full of Jerome art that they looked like miniature art museums. "These were not wealthy people collecting art as an investment but art to treasure as you would a good friend," ML said. "Artists traded among each other or bartered their work for carpentry or bookkeeping or another piece of art. It was all very personal."

Visitors to the show recognized pieces they had forgotten about and now encountered as they might a long lost friend.

"We chose the best of the best, the artists' most mature work," Karen said. "Many visitors were surprised by [the show's] very high quality. There was not a mediocre or amateurish work to be seen."

Paintings and sculptures depicted miners at work and children as they played in the crowded streets of the Mexican barrios. Viewers saw the haunting black and white photographs by Art Clark and paintings of dilapidated streets and gloomy buildings by Roger Holt that defined Jerome's ghost town years. Images of the stupendous views, quirky houses, and odd retaining walls, and photographs and paintings of hippies illustrated the restoration years. The show was a visual feast. It was easy to see why Jerome was one of the most photographed and painted small towns in America.

The Ghost of William Andrews Clark

This book began with the story of William Andrews Clark. It is fitting to end with him. This major figure in Jerome's history personifies both history *and* art.

In contemporary Jerome, few people recognize his name.

Clark was one of the richest men in the world in the early part of the twentieth century and owner of Jerome's United Verde Copper Company, the richest copper mine in Arizona.

Clark's private passion was art. He amassed one of the largest collections of art outside of a museum or university. His collection included hundreds of paintings by Corot, Degas, Monet, Van Dyck, Renoir, and Rembrandt; one hundred and fifty or so pieces of Renaissance Italian maiolica and old Delft blue and white pottery; dozens of Roman and Greek statuary; Gobelins tapestries; fine Persian rugs; and rare Belgium laces.

William Andrews Clark stands like a giant in the founding of Jerome and its legacy as an art history mecca. Clark was owner of Jerome's United Verde Copper Company, the richest copper mine in Arizona. His private passion was art. One wing of the Corcoran Gallery of Art in Washington D.C. showcases Clark's large art collection. Photo from the Herbert V. Young Collection, courtesy Jerome Historical Society (HVY-15-1).

Clark built a fifteen million dollar, 137-room, nine-story mansion on the corner of Fifth Avenue and 77th Street in New York City to house his collection. It was completed in 1911. The mansion contained four large art galleries lined with red velvet. He bequeathed a large part of his collection to the Corcoran Gallery in Washington, D.C.

I made a visit to the Corcoran Gallery in Washington, D.C., in 1992, to see this fabulous collection. It was so large that after his death in 1925, his widow Anna and their daughter Huguette, and Mrs. Lewis Morris and Mrs. Marius de Brabant, Clark's daughters from his first marriage, contributed the equivalent of nine million dollars to build a new wing at the Corcoran Gallery to showcase the collection.

French artisans were meticulously restoring the extensive gold leaf in the Louis XIV Salon Dore, which was in the midst of a million dollar renovation. The room was part of Clark's sumptuous mansion and before that it was in a French palace. The gold leaf was part of the pilasters, moldings, and cornices. The room was an elegant mixture of creamy white and gold. The ceiling of the salon was a large canvas that was painted by Jean-Honore Fragonard.

Clark willed his mansion to Huguette and four children by his former marriage. Huguette and her mother moved out. The siblings had no will to live in it or maintain it. The building sold for $3 million in 1927. The owners tore it down to make way for an apartment building.[87]

Clark's passion for art was embraced by his second wife Anna and daughter Huguette and Williams Andrews Clark, Jr., his son from his first marriage.

Anna Clark collected paintings by Cezanne and Renoir. Her other passion was chamber music. She founded the Paganini Quartet and purchased four Stradivarius instruments for its musicians.

William Andrews Clark, Jr. founded the Los Angeles Philharmonic Symphony Orchestra. He was an avid collector of books about English history and literature. He bequeathed 13,000 volumes and the building that housed them to the University of California Los Angeles (UCLA), along with an endowment of $1.5 million.

Huguette was a fine arts painter and a collector of art that included paintings by Monet and Renoir. She played the violin and purchased one of Antonio Stradivari's finest violins called "La Pucelle," or "The Virgin." The tailpiece depicts Joan of Arc, the virgin warrior.

Huguette also collected Japanese, German, and American dolls. She spent millions to commission artists to build dollhouses for them and meticulously researched and oversaw the construction of their miniature furnishings and extensive wardrobes.[88]

Huguette died in 2011 at the age of a hundred and five. She left her $300 million fortune to various parties in two very different wills, which were written late in her life and within weeks of each other. The dolls and their miniature houses, valued at $1.7 million, became part of Bellosguardo, the $85 million seaside mansion in Santa Barbara, California, that Huguette and her mother Anna once lived in. Part of the estate is slated to become an arts foundation and receive $4.5 million in cash.[89]

William Andrews Clark, unlike James Stuart Douglas, owner of Jerome's second largest mine, did not build a mansion in Jerome. When he visited, he stayed in the luxurious suites of his train. After he died, the mine that he was proudest of was sold in an ironic turn of fate to Phelps Dodge Corporation in 1935, a company that he disliked.

"The past is our future," is the motto that was adopted by the Jerome Historical Society when it was founded in 1953. In the society's Mine Museum, William Andrews Clark's contributions are minimalized. There's a photo and a few meager paragraphs. Few society board members know of his passion for art and his collection. The salesperson at the museum's gift shop did not know of him when I visited with her in 2012. "I'm just learning about Jerome," she told me.

It is sad that William Andrews Clark, founder of the twin pillars of history and art upon which contemporary Jerome is built, is so forgotten. He has become a ghost, lost in the swirl of Jerome's tourism gold rush.

Epilogue—Disconnecting from Jerome

My husband and I moved to Hines, Oregon, an urban island in the middle of a beautiful, empty, and traffic-free high desert of southeastern Oregon in 2006.

Why did we leave Jerome? We had to. We felt corralled, fenced in by the tourists that choked town during the day and the sometimes ten-minute wait to find enough of a hole in traffic to exit our street.

I was in the early stages of asthma, and Walter had emphysema. Jerome's high altitude and the smog in the valley exacerbated our conditions. We were headed into the strong currents of old age and felt inadequate to deal with them.

And we were broke. We had a lot of debt and most of our savings had evaporated in a downturn of the stock market and our own financial mismanagement.

We took the money we had left, rented out our Jerome house, and fled to Oregon.

A year later, I returned to Jerome to reconnect with my feelings of why I moved there twenty-five years ago and why I moved away.

It still felt like I had been uprooted, not just of my own roots, but strands that belong to my family and friends, and everyone else whose lives were in large and small ways influenced by my presence here. Our lives were so entwined they resembled the roots of the *Ailanthus* trees that grow so prolifically, roots that linked and spread to become one tangled, unruly forest.

The feelings of being uprooted softened with the pleasures of meals, walks, laughter, and stories of shared adventures. The warmth and welcoming of family and friends left me with an overwhelming sadness that I must still push to the back of my heart.

The overwhelming beauty of Jerome could not be avoided. From the window of the apartment that I stayed in, it looked like a quaint model-train village. Colorful little boxes, perfectly fixed up and painted, were capped by triangular roofs that were stacked and inset into the steep, burnt sienna pyramid-shaped mountains. Plum, apricot, and almond trees were in full bloom and hundreds of trees showed a blush of chartreuse. A town once denuded of vegetation had turned into a lush oasis.

I looked downhill from another window. Seventeen hundred feet below, a great cloudscape formed an abstract shadow on the floor of the Verde

Valley. The sun spotlighted canyon buttes fifty miles across the valley and turned them vivid shades of carmine. I could see the houses of Sedona, the entrances to many canyons and, above the buttes, the tops of the San Francisco Peaks. That day, veils of snow and rain showers, rainbows and clear skies could be seen in one sweep of the eyes. Few towns surpass these spectacular views that Jerome has from its mountainside perch.

When I walked uptown, bedlam reigned. I threaded my way through throngs of people on Main Street. The bump and grind of cars, trucks, and motorcycles clashed with the rock 'n' roll music that bellowed from one of the bars. The smells of car exhaust mixed with the fumes of broiled hamburgers and barbecued pork. The views were still spectacular, but it was not as pleasant to be immersed in them. The feelings of being corralled rushed right back in.

Money flows into Jerome from tourist veins that are as rich as any gold mine. Over a million visitors a year come to shop, party in the bars, gawk at the views, and hear tales of bordellos, gunslingers, and ghosts. The shops are full of art, jewelry, handmade clothing, award-winning wines, and exotic olive oils. The floor of the Bartlett Hotel, the only ruin that remains on Main Street, is filled with coins pitched by tourists at an old outhouse and toilet and rusted mining artifacts. This odd coin toss earns as much as $6,500 a year for the Jerome Historical Society.

Jerome's ghost city image remains, even though few ruins can be seen among the many restored houses and commercial buildings. The names of many businesses play on the mythology of ghosts: The Haunted Hamburger, Ghost Town Inn, the Spirit Room bar, Ghost Town Tours, and Ghost Town Gear. The annual Jerome Ghost Walk is one of the most popular events that the Jerome Historical Society produces. It draws many hundreds of people to its re-enactments of historic events.

I walked over to my old house to gather some of my favorite rocks for my new garden in Oregon. As I walked past the French windows in my kitchen, I saw our renter plopped in a chair as she drank a cup of coffee. She did not look up at me. She sat in the same place I used to love. The view from the windows widened from my bamboo patch and pomegranate tree to the wild valley of the Gulch below and to the carmine gorges thirty miles across the valley. It was a peaceful place that used to carry my daydreams to far horizons.

My heart pounded, and for a minute I could not distinguish it from the creek that pounded over the rocks below. Disoriented, I thought, "I'm one of the new ghosts that inhabit this town. I am one of the memories of home sweet Jerome."

Coda
"Thus shall you think of this fleeting world—a star at dawn, a bubble in a stream, a flash of lightning in a summer cloud, a flickering lamp, a phantom, and a dream."

—Verse from the Buddhist Diamond Sutra

Notes

1. Young, Herbert V., *Ghosts of Cleopatra Hill* (Jerome Historical Society, 1964, revised 2001), p. 33.

2. Jerome State Historic Park Exhibit.

3. Young, Herbert V, *Ghosts of Cleopatra Hill*, pp. 119, 123–24.

4. Cleland, Robert Glass, A History of Phelps Dodge 1834–1950, p. 134.

5. Klein, Robert, *James Stuart Douglas* (1868–1949), monograph. October 1995, pp. 14–15.

6. Lindberg, Paul A., "Early Proterozoic Volcanogic Massive Sulfide Deposits," Jerome, Arizona, *USA Annual Geological Society Digest 22*, 2008, pp. 601–610.

7. Clements, Eric L. *After the Boom in Tombstone and Jerome, Arizona,* University of Nevada Press, 2003, pp. 197–204.

8. *Jerome Chronicle*, summer 1985.

9. Nor was it the first time the ground shifted and destroyed buildings. An interesting paper that summarized the damage and arbitration and assessed risk for new building was done by S.D. Neely in 1995. "Potential Causes of Historical Landslide and a Probabilistic Approach to Assessing Future Risk for Development of Jerome Rest."

10. Herbert V. Young, *They Came to Jerome*, Jerome Historical Society, 1972, p. 49.

11. John McMillan interview, Jerome Historical Society archives.

12. Author interview with Paul Lindberg in 2011. Lindberg also told me that at the turn of the century there was a shaft in the basement of the newly built J.C. Penney building. The shaft was used to measure the movement of land. UVX was not even mining at that point. "Measurements taken in those years showed that the land was already slipping. On my own, I mapped two natural landslides in an area similar to Jerome's that had slipped on their own."

13. According to author conversation with Glenda Farley in January 2013, a relative of Henry M. Farley, one of two hauling contractors in the area.

14. In 1960, Mingus Union High School was established and Cottonwood joined Clarkdale and Jerome. The enlarged student body returned to the old Jerome High School in 1961. The school was closed for good in 1972 after a new high school was built in Cottonwood.

15. This estimate was based on a property survey conducted by the town of Jerome in 1981 that counted 252 buildings in Jerome and another nine buildings that represented the former Douglas properties, 190 of them private residences. By that time, some of the private residences had collapsed, so the 1953 figures are approximates.

16. The figure of how many people stayed behind has been variously represented. When I moved here in 1980, I was told fifty people stayed behind. Many tourist magazines and newspapers have repeated this number. When I interviewed family members of those who had stayed behind, as well as newcomers, and studied historical documents, I accumulated quite different figures.

17. Clark, Art, and Richard Snodgrass, *Ballad of Laughing Mountain,* Counterpoint Productions, 1957, p. 28.

18. *Jerome Chronicle*, Spring 1998, quoting article by Ralph Dighton, AP, News Features, January 16, 1946.

19. *News Bulletin,* Jerome Historical Society newsletter, 1955.

20. The owners of the Big Hole Mine were Mark Gemmill, his son Dick, and Gordon Robineau.

21. Douglas Mansion geologic display, *The Verde Independent,* April 15, 1965, and author interview with Paul Handverger, 2011.

22. Email to author.

23. Author interview with John McMillan, 1983.

24. The first officers and members of the Executive Council of the Jerome Historical Society were: President, Johnie O. Moore; Vice President, Mrs. Kathryn Beale; Second V.P., Mr. Joe Pecharich; Honorary V.P., Mr. Lewis Douglas (James Douglas' son); Secretary, Mrs. Betty Yurkovich; Treasurer, Mrs. Alberta C. Clark; Assistant Secretary, Mrs. Frances Wright. Jimmie Brewer was appointed as President of the Executive Council with members John McMillan, James Haskins, Harry Mader, Howard Rogers, Bill Wright, and Joe Pecharich. Minutes of the Jerome Historical Society, Jerome Historical Center archives.

25. The Fashion Saloon and Gambling House opened in 1903. Besides the saloon and sporting house, it had a beer and German lunch hall and bowling alley. According to the April 20 edition of the *Jerome Mining News,* it was "one of the largest and most complete establishments of its kind on the Pacific Coast, and in fact, it can be safely claimed, on this continent." In later days it became a drug store and department store.

26. In the 1980s, the Society for Creative Anachronism recreated Espejo's Spanish expedition from Hopi lands through Rattlesnake Canyon, across the Verde Valley to Jerome, complete with armor, horses, foods, weaponry, etc.

27. John McMillan interview, Jerome Historical Society archives.

28. Luke the Spook was also the name given to a B-29 Superfortress, configured to carry the atomic bomb.

29. One of these signs remains as signage for the blast furnace that sits on Main Street to the left of the amphitheater-like stone steps.

30. Author interview with Billy Watt. Many others have told me similar tales.

31. Jerome Historical Society archives, *Jerome Chronicle.* The newsletter was called the "Jerome Chronicle" or "News Bulletin."

32. Jerome Historical Society minutes, December 1953.

33. *Verde Copper News*, June 21, 1927, p. 1, Jerome Historical Society archives.

34. It should be noted that close ties existed between the town of Jerome, Jerome Historical Society, and Verde Exploration. Kathryn Beale was on the JHS board and her husband Clarence (CJ) was manager for Verde Exploration Limited and a member of the school board. JHS members John McMillan, Harry Mader, Laura Williams, and Herbert Young had worked for Phelps Dodge. Mader was Jerome's town manager and McMillan was the mayor. In later years, geophysicist Arthur A. Brant and geologist Louis Reber were members of the JHS board.

35. Most all deeds to properties sold in Jerome contain the 25-foot provision.

36. Copy of the deed is available at the Jerome Historical Society.

37. C. J. Beale died in 1972 at the age of 94. A brief good biography of him is found in Herbert V. Young's book, *Ghosts of Cleopatra Hill*, in the updated edition, on page 180. The Clarkdale athletic field was named for him, as was the main athletic field for Mingus Union High School until the school moved down to Cottonwood.

38. Photo display 2012, Arizona State Park Museum, Jerome; Diane Geoghegan, personal memorial; Rabago, *Rich Town Poor Town*, "The Millionaire and the Tamale Lady," pp. 122–129.

39. The vacuum system is now on display at the Jerome State Historic Park, a most glorious and interesting contraption.

40. According to Margaret Mason, who moved to Jerome in the 1950s and became a board member of the Jerome Historical Society.

41. http://azstateparks.com/Parks/JERO/index.html

42. GRH (full name is unidentified), "Jerome in the Spotlight," a commentary on the Gallap Report, commissioned by the Jerome Historical Society, pp. 4–5. The document is part of the archives of the Jerome Historical Society.

43. The snow totals in northern Arizona included the state record of 102.7 inches at Hawley Lake. Other totals are 99 inches at Greer, 91.5 inches at the Heber Ranger Station, 87.3 inches at Crown King, 86 inches at Flagstaff, 77 inches at Payson, 46 inches at Prescott, 40 inches at Winslow, and 31 inches at the south rim of the Grand Canyon. The Arizona one-day snowfall record of 38 inches was established during this storm at the Heber Ranger Station on December 14, 1967. Phoenix set a December rainfall record of 3.98 inches during this tempest.

44. Handverger, Paul, "Arizona's Greatest Snow Storm," *The Verde Independent*, February 11, 2008.

45. H.C. Gallap of Sedona, Arizona, and Victor H. Hogg of Lansing, Michigan. Division of Historic Development (Frank & Stein Associates, Inc.), "A Preliminary Study for the Preservation and Development of Jerome, Arizona—a National Historic Site, 1968, 10 pages. Document is part of the archives of the Jerome Historical Society. The Jerome Historical Society paid $1,000 for this study, which included many valid recommendations. Unfortunately, the study languished in the society's files and was forgotten.

46. The word "hippie" was first coined in written media by San Francisco

writer Michael Fallon in 1965 and later popularized by San Francisco columnist Herb Caen. Beatniks referred to people who were "hip" as "hipsters," and the term eventually morphed to "hippie." Neal Cassady, one of the members of Ken Kesey's psychedelic Merry Pranksters was a beatnik, the term used for counterculture types of the 1950s. As a side note, some of the Pranksters, including Cassady, came to San Miguel Allende when I lived there in 1967. I became close friends with Cassady, who took me on my first psychedelic mushroom trip.

47. RDH (name unable to be identified), "Jerome in the Spotlight" commentary on the Gallap Report, Jerome, July 18, 1968, 13 pages, Jerome Historical Society Archives.

48. Rushton, Thodore A. "Jerome's historic past faces 'long hair' presence," *Tucson Daily*, August 24, 1972.

49. Interview with Laura Williams, Jerome Historical Society archives.

50. Lease Agreement between Phelps Dodge Corporation and the Jerome Historical Society, 1973, Jerome Historical Society archives.

51. Articles of Incorporation, Jerome Historical Society archives.

52. Flier, "Jerome's 'Society Row' to Live Again," Jerome Historical Society archives.

53. Jerome Historical Society archives.

54. Monthly reports furnished by RESTOCOM are in the Jerome Historial Society archives.

55. Excerpts from RESTOCOM reports furnished to the Jerome Historical Society.

56. Margaret Mason, president of the Jerome Historical Society, September 1975 minutes.

57. Author interview with Dave Hall, with additional interviews with Richard Martin, Mimi Currier, Carmen Kotting, and Jane Moore. Dave Hall served as Jerome's fire chief from the early 1980s until June of 2001. Under his leadership, the department evolved into a modern, well-equipped, well-trained unit with a selfless team spirit that allowed it to handle various structural and brush fires during the 1980s and '90s that, in the past, might have burned large sections of town.

58. Interview with John McMillan, Jerome Historical Society archives.

59. Interview with Jane Moore, head of Planning and Zoning in the 1980s. She was vice mayor from 1982–84, elected to the Town Council from 1998–2008 and was appointed mayor 2004–06. Since 1980, she worked for Made in Jerome Pottery, which is now housed in a handsome new building on Main Street.

60. James Stuart Douglas designed a completely separate water and sewer system for the United Verde Extension mine, Daisy Hotel, and mine and office residences. These are part of Yavapai County and not part of the incorporated town of Jerome nor part of Jerome's historic district.

61. Doyle Vines, author interview. Doyle was first hired to be a part-time town crewman, then worked simultaneously as zoning administrator and building

inspector, became assistant town clerk and later, for several years, town clerk and town manager.

62. Mike Pettapiece, Toronto journalist who interviewed John McMillan in 1984. John was seventy-nine. Parts of the interview appeared in the *Jerome Chronicles* 1984.

63. Diane Peart, "A Tree Grows in Jerome," Eleventh Annual Historic Symposium, August 27, 1988, *Ailanthus Era.*

64. Richard Martin, Duke and Dorothy Cannell, "The New Chevy and Train Whistles," unpublished manuscript. Excerpted with permission.

65. *Business Wire,* November 19, 2006.

66. Sadly, the statue was stolen sometime in the 1990s.

67. Doyle Vines overall coordination and administration; Jane Moore for mapping and coordination of planning elements; Jean Amick, R.J. Amick, Pam Ballatore, Stephanie Ballatore, Lee Christensen, Mary Clark, William Clark, Roger Davis, Nancy Driver, Doug Gustafsen, Carole Hand, Lois Hayes, Mary Johnson, Marion Larsen, Katie Lee, Richard Martin, Iris and John McNerney, Mary Beth Phelps, Mark Runyan, Nancy Smith, Jon Tudan, and Jo Van Leeuwen. Photography: Tom Barber, Roger Davis, Rita Gehring, Gay Johnson, Noel Knapp, Gary Romig, Doyle Vines, and John Bell for the development work. Development of land use and circulation elements: Ed Dowling.

68. Martin, Richard, "Out in the Country," unpublished monograph on the drafting of Jerome's Comprehensive Plan.

69. *The Verde Independent,* October 7, 1983.

70. *The Verde Independent,* October 19, 1983.

71. *The Verde Independent,* November 4, 1983.

72. *The Verde Independent,* January 20 and 27, 1984; *Arizona Republic,* January 18, 1984.

73. Supplementary Report, Department of Public Safety, October 14, 1985.

74. Report made by John Brown, Special Agent, DEA, August 13, 1985.

75. Records obtained by the author from the California Bureau of Criminal Identification and Investigation.

76. Report of Investigation, Drug Enforcement Administration, August 9, 1985.

77. Faernstrom's handwritten statement that was attached to Department of Public Safety document February 25, 1985. Similar documents were obtained for others that were arrested. Author's personal archive.

78. Fred Smith, *Arizona Republic,* February 14, 1987.

79. Fred Smith, *Arizona Republic,* February 14, 1987.

80. Correspondence posted on my blogpost: http://homesweetjeromedrapaport.wordpress.com

81. Amy Waddell grew up to be a director of award-winning short documentaries. *Brothel,* her first feature-length film, is a ghost story that was shot in Jerome

and was inspired by Jerome's House of Joy, a fabulous restaurant that was converted by its owners into an antique shop.

82. In 2012, AZIC continued to sell the mercury analyzer with a slightly different name: The Jerome® Mercury Vapor Analyzer. http://www.azic.com/cs_jerome.aspx

83. Arthur A. Brant, taped interview, Jerome Historical Society archives (transcribed by Nancy Smith).

84. Lee, Katie, "The Ride," *Sandstone Seduction* (Johnson Books, 2004), pp. 185–192.

85. You can find out more about Katie Lee's books, music, videos, and activism at her website: www.katydoodit.com. "Old Jerome" is found on Kate Wolf's album, *The Wind Blow Wild,* released after her death from leukemia in 1986. You can listen to it at https://myspace.com/katewolfmusic/music/song/old-jerome-live-kpfa-berkeley-ca-29077446.

86. Demand letter, March 5, 1990, author's archives.

87. United Press, "Famous Clark Mansion, Late Senator's Hobby Brings $3,000,000 in N.Y., *Washington Herald*, February 3, 1927.

88. Dedman, Bill and Paul Clark Newell, Jr. *Empty Mansions: The Mysterious Life of Huguette Clark and the Spending of a Great American Fortune,* Ballantine Books, 2013, pp. 165–189.

89. Dedman, Bill, "Huguette Clark's $300 million copper fortune is divided up: Here's the deal," *NBC News*, September 24, 2013.

Bibliography

Books

Abbott, Lon and Terri Cook, *Geology Underfoot in Northern Arizona*. Missoula: Mountain Press Publishing Company, 2007.

Adams, Ward R., *History Of Arizona*. 4 Volumes. Phoenix, Arizona: Record Publishing Company, 1930.

Andre Baeyens, "Senator Clark, Ami de la France," and "Turning Copper into Gold," in Coyle, Laura and Dare Myers Hartwell, *Antiquities to Impressionism, The William A. Clark Collection*, The Corcoran Gallery of Art. In association with Scale Publishers, London, 2001.

Blakey, Ron and Wayne Ranney, *Ancient Landscapes of the Colorado Plateau*. Flagstaff: Grand Canyon Association, 2008.

Bourke, John. G., *General Crook in the Indian Country*. Colorado: The Filter Press, 1973.

___. *On the Border With Crook*. Lincoln: University of Nebraska Press. 1971. (Reproduced from the 1891 edition published by Charles Scribner's Sons.)

Braatz, Timothy, *Surviving Conquest: A History of the Yavapai Peoples*. Lincoln: University of Nebraska Press, 2003.

Brandes, Ray, *Frontier Military Posts of Arizona*. Globe, Arizona: Dale Stuart King, 1960.

Bristow, Allen L., Lewis H. Goddard, Ellswoth M. Schnebly, and Albert E. Thompson, *Those Early Days, Oldtimers' Memoirs*. Sedona, Arizona: The Sedona Westerners, 1975.

Byrkit, James W., *The Palatkwapi Trail*. Flagstaff, Arizona: The Museum of Northern Arizona, 1988.

Caillou, Aliza, editor, *Experience Jerome and the Verde Valley: Legends and Legacies*. Thorne Enterprises, Sedona, Arizona, 1990.

Carter, Bill, *Boom, Bust, Boom: A Story about Copper, the Metal that Runs the World*. New York: Scribner, 2012.

Cleland, Robert Glass, *A History of Phelps Dodge 1834–1950*. New York: Alfred A. Knopf, 1952.

Clements, Eric, L., *After the Boom in Tombstone and Jerome, Arizona*. Reno: University of Nevada Press, 2003.

Corbusier, William T., *Recollections of A Famous Army Surgeon and His Observant Family on the Western Frontier 1869–1886*. Globe, Arizona: Dale Stuart King, 1969.

Coyle, Laura, and Dare Myers Hartwell, *Antiquities to Impressionism, The William*

A. Clark Collection. Washington, D.C.: The Corcoran Gallery of Art, in association with Scale Publishers, London, 2001.

Dedman, Bill and Paul Clark Newell, *Empty Mansions: The Mysterious Life of Huguette Clark and the Spending of a Great American Fortune*. New York: Ballantine Books, 2013.

Forbes, Jack. D., *Apache, Navaho, and Spaniard*. Norman, Oklahoma: University of Oklahoma Press, 1960.

Gifford, E. W., *Northeastern and Western Yavapai*. Berkeley: University of California Publications in American Archeology and Ethnology. Volume 29, Number 3. Berkeley, 1932.

———.*The Southeastern Yavapai*. Berkeley, California: University of California Publications in American Archeology and Ethnology. Volume 34, Number 4. 1936.

Hicks, Peggy, *Ghost of the Cuban Queen Bordello*. Jerome, Arizona: Arizona Discoveries, 2011.

Holbrook, Stewart Hall, *The Age of the Moguls*. New York: Doubleday and Company, 1953.

Horr, David A., editor, *The Yavapai Indians*. New York: Garland Publishing, 1974.

Jacobs, Louis L., Peter J. Pilles, Jr., Pat Stein, and Robert W. Munson. *People of the Verde Valley*. Flagstaff, Arizona: The Museum of Northern Arizona, 1984.

Lew Davis, The Negro in America's Wars and Other Major Paintings, Retrospective Catalog for the art show sponsored by the Scottsdale Center for the Arts, September 13–November 13, 1990: Scottsdale, Arizona: Scottsdale Culture Council, 1990.

Malone, Michael P., *The Battle for Butte*. Seattle, Washington: University of Washington Press, 1981.

Mangam, William Daniel, *W.A Clark and His Tarnished Family*. Old Butte Publishing, 2006.

Molly, Terry, *Jerome Times: Ghosts Upon the Page*. Jerome, Arizona: Terry Molloy, 2005.

Ranney, Wayne, *The Verde Valley: A Geological History*. Flagstaff, Arizona: The Museum of Northern Arizona, 1989.

Robago, Roberto, *Rich Town Poor Town: Ghosts of Copper's Past*. Jerome, Arizona: MultiCultural Educational Publishing Company, 2011.

Ruland-Thorne, Kate, editor. *Jerome and the Verde Valley: Experience Legends and Legacies*. Sedona, Arizona: Thorne Enterprises, 1990.

Schmitt, Martin F., editor, *General George Crook: His Autobiography*. Norman: University of Oklahoma Press, 1986.

Simon, Kate. *Fifth Avenue: A Very Social History*. New York: Harcourt Brace Jovanovich, 1978.

Snodgrass, Richard, *Ballad of Laughing Mountain*, photos by Art Clark. Counterpoint Productions, 1957.

Spicer, Edward H., *Cycles of Conquest: The Impact of Spain, Mexico, and the United States on the Indians of the Southwest 1533–1960*. Tucson: University of Arizona Press, 1962.

Stevens, Robert C., editor, *Echoes of the Past: Tales of Old Yavapai, Volume 2*. Prescott, Arizona: The Yavapai Cowbelles Incorporated, 1964.

Thollander, Earl, *Back Roads of Arizona*. Flagstaff, Arizona: Northland Press, 1978.

Thoman, Konrad V., *A Camera Captures Jerome and the Verde Valley*. Cottonwood, Arizona: Marten Publications, Inc., 1971.

Wagoner, Jay J., *Arizona Territory 1863–1912*. Tucson, Arizona: University of Arizona Press, 1975.

Wahmann, Russell, *Auto Road Log* (revised edition). Cottonwood, Arizona: Russell Wahmann and Albert E. Robinson, 1991.

————. *Cleopatra's Railroads*. Jerome, Arizona: The Community Service Organization, 1975.

————. *Narrow Gauge to Jerome: The United Verde and Pacific Railway*. Jerome, Arizona: Jerome Historical Society, 1983.

————. *Verde Valley Railroads: Trestles, Tunnels and Tracks*. Jerome, Arizona: Jerome Historical Society, 1999.

Watson, Wendy M. *Italian Renaissance Maiolica from the William A. Clark Collection* (catalog of a traveling exhibition, organized by the Corcoran Gallery of Art and The Mount Holyoke College Art Museum): Scala Books, London, England, 1986.

Wellman, Paul I., *The Indian Wars of the West: Death in the Desert*. New York: Doubleday, 1954.

Young, Herbert V., *They Came to Jerome*. Jerome, Arizona: Jerome Historical Society, 1972.

————. *Ghosts of Cleopatra Hill*. Jerome, Arizona: Jerome Historical Society, 1964.

Periodicals and Newspapers

Arwood, Jim, "Jerome's Drug Conspiracy Rekindles Old Debate." *Prescott Sun*, October 16, 1985.

Bartlett, Katharine, "Notes Upon the Routes of Espejo and Farfan to the Mines in the Sixteenth Century." *The New Mexico Historical Review*, Volume 17, Number 1, January 1942.

Brothers, Frank, "Valley of Haven: The Verde." *Arizona Highways Magazine*, 1983.

Chaplin, Robert (Chappy), "Historical Notes: Geologically Speaking." *Jerome Times*, April 29, 1983.

Charnock, Richard and Steve Yozwiak, "Drug Roundup Targets Jerome Chief of Police, 2 Councilmen, 21 Others." *Arizona Republic*, October 12, 1985.

Consol, Mike, "Fear and Loathing in Jerome." *Sedona Times*, October 25–29, 1985.

Corbusier, William H., "The Apache Yumas and Apache Mohaves." *American Antiquarian*, Volume 8, 1886.

Engler, Dave, "Authorities Claim Drug Raid was a Success." *The Verde Independent*, April 16, 1986.

Fox, Margalit, "Huguette Clark, Reclusive Heiress, Dies at 104." *The New York Times*, May 24, 2011.

Graffius, Bill, "Dawn Raid Nets 21 Marijuana Valley Arrests." *The Journal*, October 16, 1985.

———. "Three Officials Resign." *The Journal*, October 23, 1985.

Handverger, Paul, "Arizona's Greatest Snow Storm." *The Verde Independent*, February 11, 2008.

Hartocollis, Anemona, "Tentative Deal in Feud over Will of an Heiress." *The New York Times*, September 21, 2013.

Holquist, Robert D., "Jerome Drug Raid Busts 23 Statewide." *The Courier*, October 13, 1985.

Isacks, Bryan, Jack Oliver, and Lynn Sykes, "Seismology and the New Global Tectonics." *Journal of Geophysical Research*, Volume 73, Issue 18, January 1968.

Jewett, Dale, "Ballatore Turns Himself in to Legal Authorities." *The Verde Independent*, October 16, 1985.

Letters to The Editor, *The Verde Independent*, October. 7, 1983; October 19, 1983; and November 4, 1983.

Lindberg, Paul A., "Early Proterozoic Volcanogic Massive Sulfide Deposits, Jerome, Arizona." *USA Annual Geological Society Digest* 22, 2008.

Lindsey, Robert, "Ghost Town That Was Restored to Life is Now in Uproar Over Raid for Drugs." *The New York Times*, January 15, 1986.

———. "Drug Scandal with an Old West Setting." *San Francisco Chronicle*, February 9, 1986.

Robertson, Jeri, "Chief Accused in Drug Trafficking." *The Verde Independent*, October 7, 1983.

———. "Jerome Drug Lab Raided." *The Verde Independent*, January 20, 1984.

Smith, Fred, "Two Resign from Jerome Council in Marijuana Case." *The Arizona Republic*, October 18, 1985.

———. "Snitch Who Set Up Drug Raid to Avoid Prison is Missing." *The Arizona Republic*, December 6, 1985.

———. "After the Bust: 'There's a Fire Burning Bright in Old Jerome.'" *The Arizona Republic*, December 22, 1985.

———. "Fugitive Informer's Offer to Testify in Drug Trials Rejected by Officials." *The Arizona Republic*, January 15, 1986.

———. "Jerome Informer Resurfaces in Jail." *The Arizona Republic*, February 14, 1987.

Stocker, Joseph, "Tumbleweed Town with a Love of Life." *Arizona Highways Magazine*, May 1976.

"The Dedication of the Episcopal Church." *Verde Copper News*, June 21, 1927, page 1. Jerome Historical Society archives.

The Jerome Chronicle and News Bulletins. Jerome Historical Society, 1953–2012.

Trullson, Barbara Nora. "Art and History Keep a Ghost Town Alive," part of an article titled "Our Most Picturesque Towns." *Sunset: The Magazine of Western Living*, February 1993.

Documents Pertinent to the Drug Raid of 1985 in Jerome, Arizona

Arrest Records for James William Faernstrom. Bureau of Criminal Identification Investigation

Disposition Reports, Department of Public Safety, October 14, 1985

Formal Complaint. Justice Court of Upper Verde Precinct, Yavapai County, Arizona, October 10, 1985.

Fowler, William S. Reports of Investigation, Department of Public Safety, Drug Enforcement Administration, State of Arizona, August 9, July 24, September 10, September 11, September 19, September 20, September 25, October 9, October 11, and October 14, 1985.

Narratives between James Faernstrom (Informant) and people arrested in the raid. Department of Public Safety, State of Arizona, October 2 and October 11, 1985.

Scientific Examination Report of Substances Obtained in the Pot Gardens, August 29 and September 13, 1985.

Search Warrant, State of Arizona, County of Yavapai, October 10, 1985.

Supplementary Investigation Reports. Department of Public Safety, State of Arizona, July 21, July 24, August 26, October 11, and October 14, 1985.

Monographs

Brewer, James W. Jr., *Jerome: Story of Mines, Men, and Money*. Southwest Parks and Monuments Association, 1993.

Gallap, H.C. of Sedona, Arizona, and Victor H. Hogg of Lansing, Michigan, "A Preliminary Study for the Preservation and Development of Jerome, Arizona—a National Historic Site. Division of Historic Development (Frank & Stein Associates, Inc.), 1968, ten pages. Document is part of the archives of the Jerome Historical Society.

Klein, Robert, "James Stuart Douglas (1868–1949)." October 1995. Jerome Historical Society archives.

Martin, Richard, "Out in the Country." Unpublished monograph on the drafting of Jerome's Comprehensive Plan, 1995.

———. "Duke and Dorothy Cannell, the New Chevy and Train Whistles," story initially published in Diane Rapaport's WordPress blog, homesweetjeromedrapaport.

McDonald, Lewis J., "Jerome Arizona," excerpted by McDonald from a Master's Thesis that he wrote entitled "The Development of Jerome, Arizona, A Typical Arizona Mining Town." Unpublished. Author's personal archives.

Neely, S.D. (P.E. Terracon), "Probabilistic Approach to Assessing Future Risk for Development of Jerome Rest Area." Terracon, Inc., Phoenix, 1995.

Piner, Judie, "Jerome Occupational Analysis." Scholarly paper for Department of Anthropology at Northern Arizona University, 1988.

Smith, Nancy, compiler, *Jerome, Arizona, A National Historic Landmark: A Design Review Handbook*. Town of Jerome, 1989.

Archives of the Jerome Historical Society

Jerome Chronicles. Newsletters of the Jerome Historical Society, 1954–2014.

Mason, Margaret, "The 1950s—Jerome in Transition." The Fifth Annual Historic Symposium.

Minutes of the Jerome Historical Society, 1953–2010.

Peart, Diann, "A Tree Grows in Jerome." Eleventh Annual Historic Symposium, August 27, 1988.

Property Surveys, town of Jerome, 1981 and 1988.

Transcribed Interviews from the archives of the Jerome Historical Society: Laura Williams, John McMillan, and Arthur Brant.

Websites

Dedman, Bill, "The Clarks: An American Story of Wealth, Scandel and Mystery," photo and videos posted: very popular TV narrative ... brilliantly and thoroughly researched ... lots of research ... good photos: storyhttp://www.msnbc.msn.com/id/35470011/ns/business-local_business/t/clarks-american-story-wealth-scandal-mystery/#.ULYycBxa6iQ;;; then good narrative in two parts

Hunter, Dana, "Oceans of Ore: How an Undersea Caldera Eruption Created Jerome." Blog: Scientific America, June 3, 2012: http://blogs.scientificamerican.com/rosetta-stones/2012/06/03/oceans-of-ore-how-an-undersea-caldera-eruption-created-jerome-arizona/

Montgomery, David (staff writer for the *Washington Post*), blog January 31, 2013: http://www.nytimes.com/2011/05/25/nyregion/huguette-clark-recluse-heiress-dies-at-104.html?pagewanted=all

SMECC.org, Interview with Evelyn Starkovitch about the closing of the radio station in Jerome in the 1940s: http://www.smecc.org/kcrj_jerome_az.htm.

Jerome Tourism Info sites

azjerome.com

Jerome Chamber of Commerce: Jeromechamber.com

Jerome Historical Society: jeromehistoricalsociety.org

Jerome State Historic Park (Douglas Mansion): azstateparks.com/Parks/ JERO/index.html

toursofjerome.com

Websites of Jerome artists and friends mentioned in *Home Sweet Jerome* (preceded by http://www.)

Anne Bassett: jeromeartistannebassett.com

Paul Nonnast—fine arts painter, sculptor and architect: flickr.com/photos/ paulnonnast/

Bob Swanson: Swansonimages.com

Dave Hall (Made in Jerome pottery): madeinjerome.com

Diane Geoghegan: dianegeoghegan.com

Kate Wolf: katewolf.com. Her song, "Old Jerome," may be heard at myspace.com/katewolfmusic/music/song/old-jerome-live-kpfa-berkeley-ca-29077446

Katie Lee: Katydoodit.com

Major Lingo: majorlingo.com

Margo Mandette and Robin Anderson: anderson-mandette.com

Mark Hemleben: www.markhemleben.com

Michael Thompson photography: michael-thompson.org

ML Lincoln: Mllincolnfilms.com *and* Wrenched-themovie.com

Noel Fray: www.theravenworks.net

Pam Fullerton: pamelajeanpress.com

Paul Nonnast—fine arts painter, sculptor and architect: flickr.com/photos/ paulnonnast/

Richard Martin and Chuck Runyon: Gulchradio.com

Scott Owens: scottowenssculptor.com

Sharon Watson and Curt Pfeffer: aurumjewelry.com

Terry Molloy: jerometimes.com/

Verde Valley Artists Cooperative Gallery: jeromecoop.com

Wylci Fables and Jore Park: Syngenie.com *and* Vizlingo.com

Appendix:
Who Lived in Jerome in 1953?

Here are the names of the people that still lived in Jerome in 1953 when Phelps Dodge closed down big mining production. They do not include the names of children that left for college and jobs elsewhere.

The list was compiled by the author with help from Diane Bell, Anthony Lozano, Jane Moore, Mickey Peterson, Roberto Sandoval, Henry Vincent, and Mike and Roberta Westcott. If anyone has a correction for this list, first names of people, names of children that are missing, or any other additions or corrections, please send them to Diane Rapaport, jhpress@centurytel.net. An attempt will be made to update the list on subsequent reprints.

One of the questions many tourists ask is "How many people stayed behind when mining stopped?" It was 132 adults and 87 children. Jerome has been continuously populated since that time and hardly qualifies for being a ghost town, as much as it may have looked like one.

John and Johanna Blazina and their children Roberta, Peter, and Elizabeth; Johanna's mother Mary Svob; and John's mother, Antonia Blazina
Clarence (C.J.) and Kathryn Beale
Mr. and Mrs. Bratnober (and children)
Nancy Bean's grandmother
Dominic and Mary Beneitone (Mickey Peterson's mom and dad)
Jimmy and Margaret Cambruzzi and their daughters Marian and Nina
Ruth Cantrell
Charles and Bruscilla (or Rosella?) Catlin
Harry and Joanne Cirata and two children, Stanley and a daughter
John Connally
Cordova
Maynard and (wife) Davenport, and three children, Maynard Jr., Richard, and Beebe Rae
Tony and Mary Dimitrov and children Louis, Frank, and a daughter
Paul and Cecelia Escobedo and children Paul Jr. and Beatriz (Bea)
Frank and Thelma Ferrell
Aurelia Contreras and Santos Gonzales (sisters)
Sabino Gonzales and his wife

Juan Atucha Gorostiaga (Father John)
Anunciata Guisti and daughter Ida
Dave Guiterrez
Geraldine Guiterrez and sons Richard and Ronnie
James and Nora Haskins
Mariano and Beatriz Hernandez and children Danny, Freddy, and Rosemary
Charles (Bonie) and Bertha Hughes
Pablo Jacquez and children, Paul Jr., Carmen, Lily, Eddy, Richard, and Henry
Emerich Kauzlaurich
Mr. and Mrs. Jampi
Tony Kauzlaurich
Nick Laddich, his mother Martha, his sister Anna, and his brother George
Dick and Chonita Lawrence, Dick's father, and Chonita's sister Pat Tissnado
Francisco and Petra Lomelli
Tony and Julia Lozano and children, Anthony Jr., Eddy, Balt, Toni, and Deanna
    and Tony's mother, Teresa Valdez, and his grandmother Solcenes
Frances and Mary Lyons
Joe Maglic
Harry and Gussie Mader
Manfreddy
Ralph and Betty Mayes and children John, Susan, and Nancy
John and Betty McMillan, daughters Patricia and Georgia, and father George Mc-
    Millan
Lewis and Irene MacDonald and children Martha and Janet
Flossie McClellan
Ray Meijilla
Pablo and Cuca Moncibaez and children Paul Jr., Vera, Arthur, Annie, Gloria, and
    Lily
Faviano Mondreal and her mother
Lola Morales who lived with her mother and grandmother and children Albert,
    Jesse, and Sandra
Mrs. Mullin
Liz Nihel and her mother Julia Vihel
Sophie Ortega and two children
Cleofas and Juan Ortiz
Mrs. Otero and her two daughters, Cookie and Carmen
Ray and Menica (Mickey) Peterson and son Andy and daughter Patricia
Joe and Elizabeth Pecharich
Mrs. Radetich and daughter Sally
Steve Radick
Ernest and Marie Ray or Alonzo and Edith Ray and several daughters
Al Robles

Mr. and Mrs. Rodriguez and daughter Angie (and other children)

Esiquia Sandoval and children, Carmen, Jesse, Robert, Josie, Beatriz, and Michael

Tony and Dora Santillan, son Ronald, and daughters Diana and Angie

Ray and Natolina Selna and children Joe and Mario

Mr. and Mrs. George Slepe, two children, and parents Jimmie Chadburn and Olivia Medina

Yee Hong Song

Leo and Beverly Sullivan and his brother Buddy

Geraldine Thomas and her father Chris

George and Bonnie Verdugo and children Bonnie, Pat, George, Ronnie, Joe, and Veronica s

Emery Vickers

Dan Vladich and his wife and their and children, Mary Lou, Dorothy, Dan and one more daughter

Paul and Mary Vognic and their son Jerry

Mr. and Mrs. Clint Wagers and three children

Andy and Laura Williams

Charles and Hazel Williams and children Eddy, Virginia, Ralph, and Larry Wycoff

Herbert V. Young

Pete and Ida Yurkovich

Index

Page numbers in **bold** indicate illustrations

V

Verde Exploration Limited (Verde Ex) 18, 20, 26, 43, 45, 68, 69
Verde Fault 15, 17
Verde Valley 26, 54
Verde Valley Art Association (VVAA), 157, 158
Verde Valley Artists 48
Vincent, Henry 53–54, 55
Vines, Doyle 60, 88, 90, 93, 95, 96
Vojnic, Jerry 86, 138
Vojnic, Paul 164

W

Water system
Collapse of 88–90
Repair of 92–93

Watson, Sharon 159
Watt, Billy 36, 49, 55, 156
Watt, Faye 49, 156
Watt, John 49, 62
Weisel, Tracy 160
White, William D. **29**
Williams, Laura 67
Wolf, Kate 170–171
Woodchute Woodworks 159
Wounded Buffalo Leathers 159
Young, Burton 22
Young, Herbert V. 13, 17, 22

About the Author

Diane Sward Rapaport's first book, *How to Make and Sell Your Own Recording*, published in 1979, revolutionized the music industry by providing information about recording and marketing indie (DIY) recordings. Over a period of 20 years, the book had five revisions and sold 250,000 copies.

A woman of many talents, Rapaport has expertise in three diverse fields: the music business, soil and groundwater contamination and cleanup, and tai chi and qigong (Chinese health exercises).

Rapaport graduated *magna cum laude* from Connecticut College in New London with a double major in English and History and earned a Masters Degree in Renaissance Literature from Cornell University in Ithaca, New York. She was an honorary Woodrow Wilson Scholar.